GAIL BUSSI

THE KITCHEN WITCH

MAGICAL AND SEASONAL BAKES TO NOURISH BODY AND SPIRIT

Hardie Grant

BOOKS

THE KITCHEN WITCH

MAGICAL AND
SEASONAL BAKES
TO NOURISH BODY
AND SPIRIT

GAIL BUSSI

CONTENTS

INTRODUCTION

*'That's the thing about magic,
you have to live like it's still here, all around us,
or it just stays invisible for you ...'*

Charles de Lint

Although all forms of cooking do possess a kind of magic – of what is often known as kitchen alchemy – to many of us, myself included, baking is the ultimate form of this art. A runny mixture of sugar, eggs, butter and flour transforms itself into a cake tasting of vanilla and sunshine; a brownish-grey, sticky lump of dough becomes, with time, a crisply fragrant loaf of just-baked bread.

Baking, in its own quiet way, returns us to ourselves and the simple joy of the moment – it is kitchen mindfulness in action! This is not just another book of baking recipes, but rather a sweet and hopefully useful exploration of how to bring magic and healing into our lives with baking, using the energies of herbs, spices, flowers, fruit and all the other ingredients that are so generously given to us by the great goddess Earth.

As a trained herbalist and flower therapist, as well as a professional baker, cook and kitchen witch, I truly believe it is in the simple moments of every day that we find the enchantment and joy: we don't necessarily need elaborate rituals or spells to access this. It's all around us, we just need to open our hearts and minds, and let the magic in!

Kitchen alchemy has been passed down through the ages, and is part of the stories and folklore of just about every country in the world; now it's a tradition we can embrace today, whoever and wherever we may be, whether you are already an experienced baker or are just starting out on this flour- and stardust-sprinkled path!

WHAT IS A KITCHEN WITCH?

'Practicality, simplicity, creativity, beauty, love –
this is the complete charge of kitchen magic,
and it is one that can change our way of living.'

Patricia Telasco

Magic in its truest sense, which implies enchantment, wisdom and transformation, is not and never has been 'something out there', something only to be attained by a select and auspicious few; kitchen witches know that it is within the context of our everyday lives and the tasks we perform in our homes that we can truly find simple magic, the kind that transforms not only ourselves but ultimately all those whose lives we touch and also the world in which we live, the same beautiful world that gives us the gifts we use in our kitchens every day.

Perhaps we should start by saying that, although for some people the word 'witch' can still be something of a loaded one, in this context it simply refers to someone who has chosen to follow and honour the simple seasons and rhythms of the year, a path that includes the domestic routines of our lives. Kitchen witches see these routines as a wonderful opportunity to tap into magic on a daily basis, right at home!

You will find more about kitchen witchcraft on the following pages, but here are some simple guidelines for your own kitchen magic path - I prefer not to use the word 'rules' since that is not what kitchen witchery is all about!

◆ Kitchen witchcraft is about embracing and enjoying the simple gifts of the changing seasons
◆ Kitchen witches focus on simplicity, and honour the Earth by not wasting her precious resources
◆ Kitchen witches work with gratitude for the abundance we have been given, and also share that abundance freely with others
◆ Kitchen witches know that we have to nourish ourselves first, in both practical and spiritual ways, in order to truly embrace our own power and grace
◆ Above all, kitchen witches enjoy their kitchens and the work they do there ... with a light and joyful heart!

BAKING WITH EARTH ELEMENTS

It's important to remember that baking invokes the magic of the four earth elements – earth, water, fire and air – and they are powerful indeed, both in everyday life and for deeper magic and rituals. The ingredients we use are part of these elements and bring our food to enchanted life, healing and nurturing us in the process.

EARTH -

represents growth, stability, abundance, prosperity, fertility and grounding. Basically just about all the food we make has some link to the earth, but foods and ingredients particularly associated with earth elements include grains (of all kinds), wheat, yeast, corn, bread, oats, peanuts, potatoes, beets, salt and beer.

WATER -

symbol of dreams, emotions, cleansing, healing and adaptability. Water ingredients include: fish, honey, milk, chocolate, sea salt, butter, cheese, apples, avocado, cabbage, lemons, melons, blackberries, thyme, tea and wine.

FIRE -

for all the warmth and passion of life, as well as courage, new beginnings and protection from negative or harmful forces. For fire elements look to ingredients like oranges, olives (and olive oil), onions, asparagus, black and cayenne pepper, chillies, coriander, garlic, ginger, mustard, nutmeg and coffee.

AIR -

symbol of dreams, communication, breath, life force and invisible energy. Air ingredients include eggs, yeast breads, grapes, mint, lavender, sage, bergamot, parsley and fruit juice.

And then there is the fifth, intangible yet wonderfully powerful element – spirit. This is the unique element that we all bring to our intentions, our actions, our purpose. Spirit is who we are, and that ultimately makes all the other elements flow together in a beautiful and delightfully magical way. Spirit is a word that, quite understandably, has different meanings for all of us, depending on our personal background, belief system and life experiences. But for me, as a kitchen witch, it's always been a spirituality based around everyday life and the simple magic contained therein, if we choose to see it.

How we get to a place of joy and magic is a completely individual journey. Perhaps I could share a little of my own path here: although I have always loved cooking and baking, I never really thought about them as being a road towards both spirit and magic, until a few years ago when I went through some really difficult and painful personal experiences. I knew I had to make some definite changes in my life (which I did, including moving to a new town and studying holistic herbalism and healing), but the most significant thing I did was to realise that it was when I was in my little kitchen that I felt most grounded and at peace. The simple act of stirring up a batch of cookies or making a loaf of bread helped my spirit come alive; I started to regain a sense of wonder and possibility, both in myself and the world around me, which is ultimately the true meaning of magic.

THE KITCHEN WITCH

BAKING WITH SIMPLICITY

*Mother Earth I honour you, and the gifts you give
in such abundance. I am truly blessed.
May all I do in this kitchen be respectful
of these gifts, and all be done in a spirit of
simplicity, grace and true gratitude.
Thank you.
And so it is.*

We live in times that offer us greater options and alternatives for our lives than ever before. There often seems to be nothing we can't do or have or be or acquire, on a physical or technological plane, but this has come at a heavy price. So many of us today are frazzled, tired, stressed and anxious all the time, both about what's happening in our lives and in the world around us. Sound familiar? It can feel as if life's an increasingly spinning wheel and we are just hanging on as best we can.

Perhaps this is one of the main reasons why so many of us are stepping back, as it were, to a simpler place and more tranquil time, a time when our homes were the quiet centre of our lives and every day unfolded in a gentle and unrushed way. Kitchen witchery is one of the most powerful ways of finding this path for ourselves, for it's a path of simplicity and calm, of order and working creatively and respectfully with the natural gifts and energies of our world.

A kitchen witch chooses ingredients with care, paying attention to how and where they were grown – preferably close to home. Choosing organic and natural is the way of the kitchen witch.

Simplicity extends to what we surround ourselves with in our kitchens too – although they do not have to be perfectly ordered, minimalist spaces – my kitchen certainly isn't! We can reduce clutter and organise our kitchens in a way that works for us but is still reflective of who we are and how we live and cook. It's a very magical choice only to buy or keep things we actually use, daily or at least frequently. (And this is written by someone who at one stage had 16 mixing bowls, of all shapes and sizes in her kitchen, all acquired because I thought I could use them, 'one day'!)

A simple, well-organised kitchen is conducive to creativity and magic on so many levels, and ensures time spent in that space will be both pleasant and productive. The recipes a kitchen witch uses also reflect healthy, earth-friendly choices, and are seasonally appropriate and affordable. Obviously, there are times we might choose to be a little more extravagant, for a special celebration perhaps, but in general we bake simply and frugally, with love and respect for the Earth and all on it, including ourselves.

BAKING WITH THE SEASONS

The world we live in is, and always has been, marked by the passage of the seasons – each with its own beauty, gifts and challenges. We also all long for connection with the Earth and with each other, and the cycles of nature remind us of that in a powerful and ancient way. The pagan calendar, also known as the Wheel of the Year, has been used for centuries as a way of marking seasonal passages and life cycles. In fact, nearly all of our traditions have their roots in the old earth wisdom, such as tracking the movements of the Moon and stars, the sun solstices, fertility rites, and so on.

As kitchen witches we can choose to honour and celebrate these seasonal shifts in a simple but meaningful way, by creating and sharing foods and feasts for each season, always bearing in mind that we not only want to thank Mother Earth for her bounty of gifts to us, but also seek to deepen our spiritual connection to these gifts, as well as to those around us.

We work with seasonal ingredients, or those associated with a particular time or festival, whenever possible; we also acknowledge the gifts of the Sun and Moon, and their influence upon us both emotionally and physically. Above all, we allow ourselves to flourish at all times of the year, bringing to both our kitchens and our lives an ancient yet fresh sense of connection and wonder.

- ◆ **WINTER** – a season of quiet introspection and rest, a time to be grounded and peaceful while we acknowledge the events and lessons of the year almost past; this time carries the cool and mystical wisdom of the Moon.

- ◆ **SPRING** – a time of awakening, of fresh purpose, growth and hope; this is the time for dreams and creativity, a time to bring new projects to life and explore our potential in all things, including in the kitchen!

- ◆ **SUMMER** – warmed by the potent energy of the Sun, summer is alive with possibility and passion, of living with abundance in the here and now.

- ◆ **AUTUMN** – as the Wheel of the Year slowly turns, so too should we start to prepare for changes, while we also celebrate the harvest we have been given; it's a time for gratitude, but also for sharing our many blessings and lessons.

There are eight major festivals celebrated during the Wheel of the Year:

Samhain (Halloween):
31 October

Yule:
21 December, the Winter Solstice

Imbolc (Candlemas):
2 February

Ostara:
21 March, the Spring Equinox

Beltane:
1 May

Litha:
21 June, the Summer Solstice

Lammas:
1 August, traditionally the harvest festival

Mabon:
21 September, the Autumn Equinox

MAGICAL TOOLS

✴ UTENSILS

As regards a witch's kitchen utensils, there are only a few basic things to remember. Firstly, try to use only steel, copper or glass for saucepans and the like – aluminium is generally cheaper but has fewer magical qualities and can leach into foods. For bowls I recommend glass or ceramics. All of these materials carry strong earth energies of stability and abundance. The same applies to baking pans and dishes you use in the oven.

You will also need a mortar and pestle – the ultimate kitchen witch accessory! Yes, you can still use an electric grinder or blender, but there's something about grinding spices and herbs in a mortar and pestle that is truly magical.

You will need wooden (or bamboo) spoons – a few of them, in different sizes – and also a spatula or two. And knives – another essential witchy tool ... I have several, small and large, and would urge you to buy the best you can afford: with knives, cheaper is definitely not better, as they will not get the job done as well or as effectively.

No kitchen is complete without a broom – obviously for cleaning and clearing up debris on a daily basis – but for a magical note you might like to have a separate, smaller broom too. Mine is around 30 cm (12 in) long, with a carved wooden handle and natural reed bristles; I keep it solely for magical/ritual purposes, and have tied its handle with thin silver and leather cords to which I have attached a few clear crystals such as amethysts, for absorbing negative energies and promoting joy and harmony, both in the kitchen and in my home. I like to symbolically sweep my countertops and kitchen table at least once a day with this little broom: it clears and cleans both psychic and physical debris.

✴ KITCHEN ALTAR

A kitchen altar may be both small and simple, but it's an important part of the magical kitchen, as it is a gentle, significant reminder of the powerful energies right here in our kitchens, and the gifts of the Earth that we use here. I would suggest using a small tray or flat basket to begin with, something that fits comfortably on a shelf or windowsill – or on your kitchen table, if you have space for that. Any kitchen altar should be out of reach of small children and pets.

A candle – a simple white pillar candle is best – should be at the centre of your altar. It also represents the fire element and can be surrounded by symbols of the other elements – crystals or pebbles for earth, a feather for air and a small dish of salt water. The rest of the altar is very much a matter of personal choice – a small vase of flowers or herbs to mark a particular season, pictures that are meaningful to you – especially of those who have cooked and baked with you over the years. I always keep a tiny photo of both my mother and great aunt on my altar, since these ladies played such a significant part in my life on every level, and I choose to remember and honour them in this way. I also have a tiny owl (for wisdom) and a small carved wooden angel, gifted to me by a long-lost friend. You can add/change items on your altar as you feel inspired to do so.

KEEPING A KITCHEN GRIMOIRE

You probably know that journal keeping has long been acknowledged to be a powerful tool for personal growth and self-awareness; I first read *The Artist's Way* by Julia Cameron over 20 years ago and still credit it with giving me the insight and courage to start writing books! But a kitchen grimoire (also sometimes known as a Book of Shadows) is equally valuable to us as kitchen witches – not just as a place to record recipes and kitchen experiments, but also as a uniquely personal record of our own magical journey, both in the kitchen and beyond.

When we bake, things often come up in our soul and spirit – for example, a recipe may make us remember a particular person or time in our life. Your kitchen grimoire is the place to record that, as well as any insights and changes we choose to acknowledge; it's a place for special thoughts and quotes that have touched us, dreams, ideas for rituals … Keep your grimoire in an accessible place – mine is on a shelf with a few much-loved and well-used cookbooks. And don't be too distressed if it gets a few food spills on the pages – your kitchen grimoire is a working, doing book, above all! We've included some pages at the back of the book which can be used for these sorts of thoughts and act as a stepping stone to your own dedicated kitchen grimoire.

BEFORE YOU BEGIN ...

Before we bake – indeed, before we undertake any magical undertakings in our lives – there are a few simple steps that will enhance and bless our actions and help us to stand in our magic ...

An important lesson: the foods we prepare are an outward reflection of how we are feeling, both emotionally and physically. There are going to be times when we are in our kitchens feeling angry, tired, depressed or anxious about life ... and in order to ensure that any negative energies are not transferred to the food we are preparing, there are a few basic ways we can bring ourselves back to a calmer, more joyful state of mind.

◆ We can use a simple-to-make purifying and blessing spray for the kitchen – to make this, half-fill a small spray bottle with distilled water, then add 120 ml (4 fl oz/½ cup) of rose water and 5 drops each of lavender and neroli essential oil. Shake well, then add a few drops of vanilla extract; use this spray lightly around the corners and countertops of your kitchen.

◆ First, we need to ground ourselves in the moment: if possible, light a small lavender or frankincense candle, or add a few drops of the essential oil to a small burner. (Both these oils have calming and uplifting properties.) Take off your shoes and stand facing the candle, or near an open window. Drop your shoulders and press your feet firmly into the ground, feeling the earth supporting and holding you. Breathe in through the nose slowly, then out through the mouth, three times. Allow negative energies to drain away into the earth and feel a new sense of joy and peace.

◆ Next, we need to set our intentions. Yes, we have decided to bake something, but with what intention. Are we making it for ourselves, for others, with a particular purpose or goal in mind, or just because we feel called to bake something in this moment? We can set our intention simply by thought, or by saying a few words that clarify this.

◆ The practical level includes gathering together everything we need to create our baked magic. This includes ingredients, utensils, baking dishes, recipe book, and so on – the kitchen witch is always well prepared and (hopefully!) never find themselves missing a crucial ingredient at the wrong moment.

◆ When preparing our recipe it's very important to remain in each moment as we work through it step by step, not allowing ourselves to be distracted by thoughts that either leap ahead or wander off at a tangent. Just by being fully present, action by action, we can turn the simplest activity into a magical and energised one.

◆ While our baked goods cook, we have an opportunity to sit and reflect – hopefully in your favourite, comfortable kitchen chair. Taking a few moments for simple reflection is a gift of well-being we can offer ourselves every day; this is also the perfect time to write in your magical kitchen journal or grimoire.

◆ While waiting for our bakes to cook, we can also clean and reset. Remember to sweep in small circles clockwise when you are looking for positive and new energies, and anti-clockwise when you want to remove negative or problem vibes of any kind. (This also applies when you are stirring batters or other food mixtures.) You can also sweep the kitchen floor (using a larger broom) from the centre outwards in ever-expanding circles – this has the same effect of sweeping away any bad or unhelpful energies.

- Finally, we need to conclude by honouring the results of our kitchen work - even when, as sometimes happens, they turn out less successfully than we had hoped. The very fact we are able to buy (or grow) ingredients, and that we have a kitchen to work in, with heat and light and the other things we need, is itself a cause for celebration and gratitude. When the baking is done (and the kitchen cleaned!), light a fragrant rose, jasmine or geranium candle and say the following words softly:

Blessed be my kitchen.
Blessed be the creations of my hands,
and the ingredients that come
from this beautiful Earth.
May I always share and honour
these blessings,
and sweet magic be part of my life,
now and always.
And so it is.

✳ MAGICAL PURIFYING KITCHEN BLENDS

To make our kitchens even more magical it's often a good idea to bring in some kitchen 'aromatherapy', by creating fragrant blends to add to candles, incense or simmer pots - which is just a pot of simmering mineral water to which you add a little herb and spice magic!

If you want a sense of peace/calm in your kitchen (and in yourself!) - particularly if there have been problems or discord in the home - combine the following: 60 ml (2 fl oz/¼ cup) of sweet almond oil, 4 drops of lavender essential oil, 3 drops of frankincense oil, and the dried and grated zest of 1 lemon. Mix well and store in a small, dark glass bottle; add a few drops of this purifying and uplifting oil to a small burner or simmer pot as suggested above.

For joy and protection in the kitchen, follow the recipe above but substitute the lavender and frankincense for 4 drops each of rosemary and thyme oil and 2 drops of mint oil; the lemon zest can still be included.

THE KITCHEN WITCH

GLOSSARY OF INGREDIENTS

The following is a list of many of the everyday ingredients we use for baking; it's by no means complete, but serves as an introduction to the ones we are likely to use most frequently and also provides lots of ideas about the magical and healing properties of these particular baking ingredients.

It's good to pause for a few moments before we bake or cook, and thank the foods for the energies they bring to us; I like to arrange the ingredients I am going to use on a suitable tray (actually this is a good basic kitchen practice, anyway – known as mise-en-place) and say the following short blessing/mantra:

I/we am/are blessed by this food.
We are truly blessed by the gifts given to us
by our abundant and magical Earth.
May our spirits always remain grateful.
Thank you. Thank you.
And so it is. So it always will be.

SPICES

Most spices are available either whole or in ground form; it's great to grind your own spices in a mortar and pestle but often easier to buy them in a ready ground form. Whatever you choose, please remember that spices do lose their fragrance and power after a while – most should be used up within a year; always keep them in glass jars, with tight-fitting lids, in a cool, dark place away from direct light.

✳ ANISE

Little seeds with a delicate aniseed/liquorice flavour; they are sold whole or ground. Wonderful when used to flavour breads, cookies, cakes or desserts; traditionally reputed to ward off nightmares and other fears, and to help with protection, divination and creating good luck. Star anise, which is a different spice, also has similar properties – it is sold whole and should be crushed before a little is added to your recipe. Alternatively, the whole seed pods can be soaked in the liquid used for a recipe, then strained out; they will have perfumed the liquid with their unique and delicious scent and taste.

✳ CARDAMOM

Used worldwide for baking spice recipes and as a key ingredient in chai, the seeds are available whole or crushed/ground; I prefer crushing them myself just before use as that way none of the unique, warm flavour is lost. Cardamom is reputed to bring about clarity and an upliftment of

the heart and spirit and is also linked to creating greater love and passion in our lives. It works well with fruit dishes and, strangely enough, chocolate.

✳ CINNAMON

Probably the most basic and widely used baking spice, cinnamon is powerful and has been used since ancient times for creativity, healing, purification and protection in all aspects of life. Cinnamon has such a strong affinity for baked goods (of all kinds) and also with creamy puddings; it should be sprinkled on any suitable recipe when you need to add a dash of spiritual power, courage and deeper creativity. And, of course, the simplest way to access its magic is to sprinkle it on your first morning coffee!

✳ CLOVES

Best bought whole and then ground just before use, otherwise they lose their distinctive and fresh aroma and taste. A

very familiar addition to holiday baking and spice mixtures, cloves should be used in moderation, otherwise they can tend to dominate; they are reputed to be powerful at clearing negative energies and creating greater harmony, both personally and within groups. A spice for friendship and attracting love and prosperity, cloves work particularly well in fruit dishes of all kinds and they have a special affinity with apples – try adding a little ground cloves to apple pies or desserts.

✳ GINGER

Another traditional and popular baking spice, ginger can be bought fresh, in dried and ground form, or as pickled/candied ginger. If you are using fresh ginger, the roots should be peeled and then finely chopped/grated. (They do pack quite a powerful punch, so should be used with restraint!) Dried ground ginger is readily available and adds its magical and healing properties to all kinds of baking; it's great for boosting your personal power and well-being on every level and also inspires passion – useful to know!

✳ NUTMEG

Nutmeg is another familiar spice that's been around for a very long time, and is used widely in Middle Eastern and Indian cuisine; it's sold both ground and whole, but is best if freshly ground before being used, as it loses its potency quite quickly. A magical spice, nutmeg is linked to prosperity, good luck and protection on both a physical and emotional level. It's delicious sprinkled on custards and baked puddings or added to fruit or spice cakes.

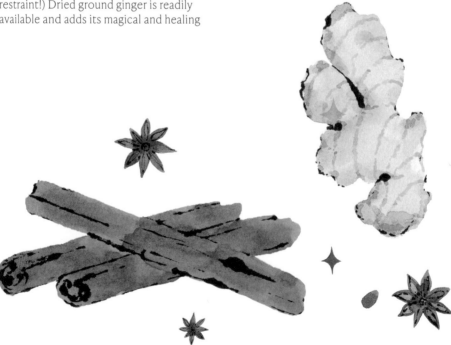

✴ PEPPER

Probably one of our most familiar spices, used in or on so many foods; it's obviously used in moderation for some savoury baked recipes but surprisingly it's also good (in moderation) when combined with chocolate and some soft fruits! Pepper has been used magically to remove jealousy and general negative energies, while simultaneously increasing personal strength and confidence. A mix of ground black peppercorns with equal quantities of dried chilli powder, paprika and ground cumin not only makes a delicious addition to savoury baked recipes but can also be used as a protective powder for your kitchen and other spaces in your home – sprinkle it in the corners of your rooms, but only out of reach of small children and pets.

✴ SAFFRON

Saffron, the dried stamens of the saffron crocus, is an ancient spice – it's part of much ancient mythology, from the Egyptians and Greeks onwards – and is reputed to help increase energy and psychic powers and dispel sadness with its bright sunny colour. It's certainly not the cheapest of spices, but a little goes a long way and it gives a lovely, delicate flavour to baked goods, in which it has been traditionally used for centuries. Just a note: some people substitute the cheaper alternative of turmeric, but it's definitely not the same in terms of flavour.

HERBS

There are so many herbs for magical kitchen purposes, but here I have concentrated on some of the most popular for sweet and savoury baking; they are also fairly easy to obtain or grow yourself. In general, I prefer to use fresh herbs wherever possible, but there are times when that isn't practical for a number of reasons. Don't worry, though, as dried herbs also work well magically – in fact, some herbs like rosemary and sage actually become more potent when dried! Normally, if a recipe calls for fresh herbs and you need to substitute with dried herbs, use about half as much – one tablespoon as opposed to two, and so on.

✳ BASIL

Basil (in all its wonderfully fragrant forms) is an ancient herb that is traditionally linked to magical protection of all kinds, and the removal of bad vibes! In fact, it was known as 'the witch's herb' and should be used whenever you want to encourage positive energies, abundance and happiness in general. Basil is mainly used in savoury baking but can also be added in small amounts to cakes and cookie batters. Alternatively, add a few dried leaves to protection powders, incense mixtures and the like, to bring its magic right into your kitchen or home!

✳ GARLIC

Although not always considered a herb, garlic is such a powerful kitchen witch ally that I can't leave it out! Obviously mainly used in savoury baking, particularly for breads, buns and muffins of all kinds, garlic is credited with powers ranging from easing negativity and depression to increasing strength and courage. Just hanging a string of garlic bulbs in your kitchen can be magical, and apparently also helps to keep unwanted visitors away! Adding garlic to salt is a great way of bringing its magic into your baking – and your kitchen.

✳ LAVENDER

Probably – and justifiably – one of the most loved and recognised herbs/flowers in the world. Both the leaves and flowers can be used in the kitchen, dried or fresh; the dried are stronger. (If you buy dried lavender for cooking, please be sure it's culinary grade.) Lavender is full of magical oils that help heal both body and mind, and it's a major calmative when life is just too much for us to cope with; it's also excellent for headaches and for helping us to get to sleep. A little lavender oil sprinkled on a candle will bring a sense of calm (and also a delightful perfume to your kitchen). Just remember that it's also a deceptively powerful herb, so less is definitely more when it comes to baking.

✳ LEMON BALM

Sacred to the goddess Diana, and used over 2,000 years ago in Greece, lemon balm has long been used as a healing herb as well as for love magic and (apparently) for promoting a long and healthy life. Today it's used in aromatherapy for easing anxiety and depression, and as a general nerve tonic. Many of us probably think of it as an ingredient in herbal teas, but it can also be used to good effect in baking; the leaves can be chopped finely and added to batters, or can simply be spread under a bread or cake mixture before baking.

✳ MINT

It's hard to know where to begin with the healing and magic properties of mint – there are so many; its bright and refreshing scent and flavour cools, calms and protects both body and mind. It's also a highly protective herb and can be used to remove negative energies, both personally and in your surroundings. Use mint (sparingly) in

baking and especially in recipes that include berries, chocolate, citrus or stone fruits like peaches. Adding a few fresh mint leaves to a glass of mineral water makes a cooling and uplifting drink; you can also add mint to other herb or black teas.

✳ OREGANO

Popular with the Greeks and Romans as a herb for love and fidelity, and for increasing happiness and peace at home. It helps with anxiety and fears of all kinds, real or imagined, as well as improving concentration. In general, oregano is only used in savoury baking, especially breads, pies and pastries – it's also fabulous when combined with tomatoes or cheese. Use both the dried or fresh herb with abundance in your kitchen, and hang a bunch of dried oregano over your kitchen door for both protection and good health.

✳ ROSEMARY

Such a beautiful herb – to grow, to savour, to enjoy on every level. (And yes, it does help to improve cognition and memory!) Use it in your cooking to add magical flavours and protection from both physical and emotional dangers. The finely chopped leaves can be used either fresh or dried, but always with caution, since this is a really powerful herb with the potential to become overwhelming. The flavour works well in breads and other baked goods, as well as desserts; it also makes a wonderful herbal syrup for this purpose. Just keeping a few sprigs of fresh rosemary on your kitchen table or windowsill will lift your spirits and sharpen your focus; it's also one of the traditional herbs for remembering

ancestors and those loved ones who have passed on.

✳ SAGE

There are many kinds of sage but for our purposes we are looking at the familiar garden sage, which also has many traditional applications for medicine, food and magic. White sage has traditionally been used in burning rituals for purification, divination and clearing energy; ordinary sage can be used for this too, and added to incense mixtures, but I prefer to use it more simply, in recipes of all kinds, or by adding it to herb pillows or bundles. Sage will cleanse and protect your kitchen (or indeed other rooms in your home); it also helps us with our dreams and wishes – apparently, if you write your wish on a sage leaf and then burn it, the wish will come true!

✳ THYME

This herb, with its fragrant little leaves and tiny flowers, comes in many culinary and medicinal variants – my particular magical favourite is lemon thyme, which makes a wonderful addition to all kinds of baked goods, especially breads and cakes. Thyme is a powerful herb with strong healing qualities on both the physical and emotional level; it's also credited with increasing courage and mental strength and has been used over the centuries for this purpose. Making herbal tea with dried or fresh thyme leaves will help you release the past and clear emotional blocks of all kinds. When combined with lavender or rosemary it makes a powerful herbal mixture for herb bundles and incense, and will remove negativity from any space.

NUTS, SEEDS & DRIED FRUIT

✳ ALMONDS

A really versatile and popular nut that is available in many forms – whole, chopped, ground (almond flour); this is a nut I would never be without in my kitchen, as I use it in cookies and cakes, as well as in its ground form to make wonderful treats like macarons. Almond trees have always held magical powers, and the same holds true for their small nuts, which can be used to increase prosperity, create powerful love bonds and also to help with greater intuition and psychic powers.

✳ COCONUT

Available in many forms: whole coconuts, coconut milk or cream, shredded coconut, coconut flour ... and more! Traditionally linked with protecting the home and the people within, this is a very feminine nut – with lots of pure moon energies. You can add pure coconut water to cleaning products for the kitchen, as it increases both the purification and cleansing of spaces.

✳ DATES

These sweet and sticky fruits have been around since (almost) time began; sacred in Babylon, Persia and ancient Greece, dates were used as offerings to the gods and linked to the afterlife and reincarnation. They are used in lots of baking recipes, especially cakes, tea breads and puddings; try and use them as fresh as possible, and if you can find Medjool dates they are particularly sweet and delicious!

✳ HAZELNUTS

Like almonds, hazelnuts (filberts) have been popular in baking recipes down the years; they can be used whole, chopped up or as hazelnut flour. For such a small, round nut they have a lot of mystical powers and are sacred to the Norse god, Thor. Eating hazelnuts is said to increase your psychic

powers and intuition, and also enable you to see faeries – who are apparently also very fond of these nuts! If you string hazelnuts on a thin cord, or add them to a kitchen altar, they will definitely protect your home and increase its magic possibilities.

✴ PECANS

Widely used in baking, pecan nuts can substitute for walnuts – although walnuts have a slightly sweeter taste. They have long been seen as a symbol of success and financial abundance; add a few whole pecans to magic bags and offerings to ensure continuous success in your work and business.

✴ POPPY SEEDS

Available as tiny dried seeds or as a paste, and used widely in breads and traditional baked goods of all kinds. These seeds are sacred to many gods and goddesses, in particular Demeter and Persephone, and they have long been associated with kitchen witches and magic of all kinds. Enjoy them liberally on food, because they promote calm, serenity and good luck; poppy seeds should be included in Samhain cakes and cookies, as a sign of respect and love for your ancestors.

✳ RAISINS

Raisins are, obviously, dried grapes and as such carry the energies of this amazing fruit – full of spiritual power, connection and prophetic dreams. They work well in recipes linked to moon magic and deities and are also a symbol of abundance.

✳ SESAME SEEDS

We are probably all familiar with bread or rolls sprinkled with sesame seeds – these tiny, creamy seeds may be small but they pack quite a punch of flavour! They are particularly sacred in the East, where it is believed they increase and strengthen our life force and inner powers. They are linked to greater prosperity and good fortune, and to the pursuit of justice. Sprinkle the seeds on savoury breads and pastries or add to cookies and cakes for a subtle touch of magic. If you combine roasted sesame seeds and sea salt, you have a Japanese mixture called 'gomasio'; this is traditionally sprinkled on hot dishes, salads, noodles, and the like.

✳ SUNFLOWER SEEDS

Not surprisingly, these striped seeds are full of the Sun's bright energy, and as such make a positive and happy addition to recipes such as breads and muffins; use them to encourage greater prosperity and confidence. The sunflower is associated with the Crown chakra and for this reason is linked to psychic awareness and growth.

✳ WALNUTS

These nuts, with their distinctive, slightly sweet flavour, can be used either chopped or ground; they are added to all kinds of traditional baked goods and are reputed to bring about good fortune, protection and increased fertility! One note of caution – these nuts have a high oil content and can become rancid quite quickly, so check before buying/using them. A good way of preventing this is to keep the bags of nuts in the freezer and simply defrost well before use.

FLOWERS

This is just a brief list of some of the edible flowers that can be used either in baked goods or as decoration. Obviously, it's important to ensure that the flowers you use are non-toxic and have been grown organically, without the use of pesticides or other harmful chemicals. Always cross-check any edible flower with an ID guide to be sure you have the correct variety.

✳ CALENDULA (POT MARIGOLD)

The bright, orange-yellow petals can be included in baked mixtures or used to add colour to icings and decorations. Calendula has lots of very positive energies and is linked to creativity and healing.

✳ GERANIUM

Scented geraniums, which come in a number of varieties – the most popular being rose- and lemon-scented – are truly wonderful in the kitchen and beyond; they create a sense of well-being, calm and peace. The fresh leaves can be used to line cake tins (pans) before adding the batter, and they can also be very finely chopped and added to bread and cake mixtures. The dried leaves make a beautiful and peaceful addition to magical mixtures of all kinds, especially those used for cleaning and purification purposes.

✳ HONEYSUCKLE

The flowers can be used as decoration, or they can be steeped in water overnight, and the resulting fragrant liquid then strained and added to cake mixtures, frostings, and so on. Honeysuckle brings good luck and increased vitality, both mental and physical.

✳ JASMINE

A flower with a hauntingly beautiful fragrance, jasmine increases harmony and tranquillity, and can also be used for meditation and spirit work. The flowers can be used in baking in the same way as honeysuckle, see above.

✳ NASTURTIUMS

Both the leaves and the brightly coloured blooms of this pretty garden flower are edible but also quite strongly flavoured, so a little goes a long way! Magically speaking, the nasturtium is linked with positive energies and new direction, helping us to find greater creativity and courage in our lives. These flowers are perfect for all kinds of kitchen witchery and are especially great when used in salads and fruit dishes, but you can also add a few chopped blossoms/leaves to baked goods such as cakes, breads and muffins as well as chilled desserts. A few whole blossoms can be used to decorate a simple cake or pie for a joyful and positive statement!

✳ ROSE

Probably the most beautiful and loved flower since ancient times, roses have almost too many magical and healing properties to list: they are a powerful symbol of love, self-esteem, beauty, harmony, sexual connection, creativity and more! I love adding the fragrance of roses to many sweet recipes, including cakes, cookies, creamy desserts, custards and cheesecakes. Culinary rose water is an absolute must in the witch's kitchen: please buy the best quality you can find, and use it sparingly, as otherwise the flavour can be a little overpowering.

✳ VIOLETS

Violets/Violas (also pansies): all these flowers have similar magical and spiritual qualities, which include the bringing of calm and peaceful thoughts, and creating inspired ideas (pansies' name comes from the French 'penser', to think.) Violets were much loved in Victorian times, and often used to decorate cakes and puddings; the fresh blossoms can be used or they can be crystallized for this purpose, by using a small paintbrush to lightly coat the flowers with a thin layer of beaten egg white, and

then sprinkling the blooms with icing sugar. (This technique can be used for single beautiful rose petals, too.)

FRUIT & VEGETABLES

✳ APPLES

A fruit with a truly long history, apples
are a part of mythology in many cultures;
they are ruled by the goddess Venus,
but are also sacred to many other gods
and goddesses. They are also a favourite
fruit of witches, especially at Samhain
and Halloween, for apples are linked to
ancestors and those who have passed
from this Earth before us. Eating an apple
is said to open us up to communication
with the spirit world, as well as creating
greater clarity in our minds. There are
so many apple varieties out there for us
kitchen witches to explore and enjoy –
and they are wonderful in baked goods
of all kinds, obviously. However, we can
also access their ancient magic by simply
floating apple slices in jugs of cold water
or iced tea, or by adding the dried peel of a
beautiful red apple to purification blends,
herbal washes or incense mixtures.

✳ BANANAS

Another fruit linked to fertility and passion
– perhaps not surprisingly when you
consider the shape! Sacred to Venus, and
also linked to prosperity and protection.
Apart from their many uses in baked goods,
bananas also make an excellent and healthy
quick snack, and should always be part of
your magic fruit bowl.

✳ CARROTS

Not really helpful when it comes to seeing
in the dark, but carrots do have some good
energies – including, apparently, the ability
to incite passion and lust … who knew?
Perhaps that's why carrot cake is often
called passion cake! Of course, carrots do
have lots of masculine properties and are
sacred to Mars, the god of war. If you need
to spice up your love life or are looking to
increase fertility, baked goods like carrot
bread or muffins are the way to go.

✳ LEMONS

Probably one of the most magical fruits of all, and much loved by kitchen witches over the centuries, lemons have such powerful cleansing and protective properties they should be used as often as possible in all our kitchen work. Obviously, the grated rind/juice of fresh lemons can be added to many different recipes, both savoury and sweet, but sliced lemons make a wonderful and purifying addition to teas and drinks of all kinds. Add fresh lemon juice to cleansing washes and simmer pots for the kitchen or elsewhere in your home; dried lemon slices also make a powerful and protective addition to herbal wreaths or magic blends.

✳ ORANGES

A fruit of the Sun, warming and uplifting with its colour, fragrance and taste. Oranges cleanse and purify both body and spirit, and the fresh juice or dried peel can be added to drinks and teas to increase energy. Dried orange and lemon peel, when combined with a vanilla pod (bean), make a wonderful and simple incense that will bring about warm feelings of friendship, connection and peace.

✳ PASSION FRUIT

Unsurprisingly, this knobbly, little, purple fruit is linked to love, friendship and general good feelings all round; it's sacred to Venus and full of feminine energies. Add it to anything you are making for loved ones, for happy and peaceful vibes. It also helps with dreams, divination and meditation. I love making simple passion fruit syrup and using it to drizzle over cakes, ice creams, meringues and other sweet treats.

✳ PEACHES

A feminine fruit full of love, spirituality and the granting of wishes. Much revered in Asian cultures as a sign of purity and longevity, serve peach desserts to create greater love and affection between partners or family members.

✳ PLUMS

Long a part of Oriental mythology plums are considered to be a symbol of wisdom and longevity, and also have strong relaxing and spiritual properties. Serve in baked goods when you want to increase someone's interest or passion.

✳ PUMPKINS

In South Africa, where I grew up, pumpkins are mainly considered a vegetable served with meat and other savoury dishes, but, of course, they are so much more than that. Not just for Halloween – although pumpkins do have a strong afterlife connection – they also make a delicious addition to pies, cakes and cookies, and are linked to healing and feminine magic, being ruled by the Moon. Add dried pumpkin seeds to any magic mixes to bring about greater prosperity and abundance in your life.

✳ RASPBERRIES

Small, delicious fruits that pack a powerful punch in terms of magic, raspberries can be used in all kinds of spellwork and rituals for protection, greater energy and love; they are also said to increase fertility. Simple raspberry syrups can be drizzled over pancakes, waffles and other baked goods to increase bonds of love and friendship, between partners or family.

✳ STRAWBERRIES

Another fruit sacred to Venus, these little heart-shaped berries carry lots of love and passion energies, as well as helping us achieve success and luck. The leaves can be dried and added to magic mixes or rituals for abundance and good fortune. Strawberries help us move from our heads to our hearts, and create a life centred around love, empathy and compassion.

HONEY, SUGAR & OTHER SWEETENERS

✴ HONEY

Honey is one of the most ancient foodstuffs around. It's a sacred gift from the bees, who themselves are fairly magical little beings and have long been seen as messengers from worlds beyond our sight. Plus, honey is simply delicious and can be used in so many ways in our kitchens: add it to all kinds of recipes for a dollop of healing, happiness, prosperity and spirituality. Faeries love it too, and if you leave a small dish of honey out overnight in your kitchen they will thank you for it, and leave some small gift in return, so old legends go. Try adding a spoonful of honey to teas and herbal drinks, or sprinkle it on porridge or muesli for a morning lift. One of my favourite things is honey butter, which is easily made by combining softened butter with a few teaspoons of your preferred honey; beat till creamy and smooth, then serve over pancakes, scones and toast.

✴ MAPLE SYRUP

Maples are very magical trees and the syrup tapped from their sap carries all the same qualities, such as abundance, long life, prosperity, and attracting love and fidelity. Real maple syrup is not cheap, unfortunately, but please don't use imitation maple syrup, which is just golden (light corn) syrup with artificial flavouring added.

✴ SUGAR

Obviously a pretty important ingredient in sweet baking of all kinds, sugar comes in many forms: regular, brown, caster (superfine), icing (powdered). It sometimes gets a bad rap and certainly we should all try and limit our sugar intake to reasonable levels, but I still prefer using it to the artificial sweeteners and sugar substitutes out there – although for some people they are necessary for health reasons. Basically, sugar sweetens life on many levels, and it can be used in magical and love rituals for this purpose; it's also a protective food, sacred to the Hawaiian god Kane, and helps to ward off evil forces.

FLOURS & GRAINS

According to tradition there were seven sacred grains in ancient times: rice, barley, corn, oats, millet, rye and wheat, and over the centuries these grains have kept entire civilisations nourished and healthy. They are an intrinsic part of much of our cooking/baking today, too, and continue to make healthy magic in the witch's kitchen!

✳ BARLEY

One of the oldest grains, and traditionally linked to harvest celebrations, barley was used for protection, love, grounding and healing emotional issues. It's also excellent for increasing prosperity, especially when mixed with a little salt and sprinkled around your workspace or property.

✳ CORN

Either in its original form or ground up as cornmeal or cornflour (cornstarch), corn is a very magical grain and can be used in all kinds of rituals and celebrations, particularly those related to the harvest. Corn signifies abundance and prosperity, and a little cornmeal added to magic powders will bring about greater luck and protection from negative forces. Cornmeal and cornflour are also naturally gluten-free.

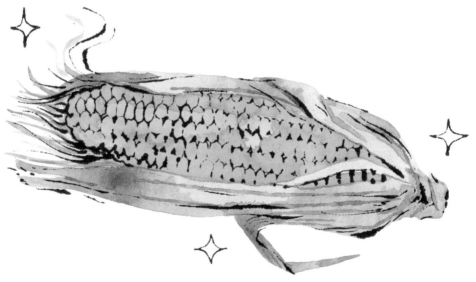

✴ OATS

Oats, either whole, rolled or ground into oatmeal, have been a kitchen staple for thousands of years; this grain is full of feminine energies and is also linked with prosperity, fertility and passion – possibly where the phrase 'sowing your wild oats' came from? Oats are particularly yummy in breads and cookies; make simple oat breads for harvest festivals, and to honour the goddesses of the Earth and invoke blessings for your life.

✴ RICE

The staple, everyday food for so many of the Earth's peoples, rice is a truly versatile grain with lots of practical and magical applications. The culinary uses are fairly obvious, but what you may not know is that rice is linked to good luck and abundance in all areas of life and is said to remove evil and negative forces from your home. Foods made with rice help keep us grounded and emotionally present. Add rice to magic mixes and spells to create protection and healing.

✴ RYE

Rye flour is widely used to make different kinds of bread; use it in baked goods to increase feelings of love and connection between lovers, friends and family.

✴ WHEAT

The flour we are probably all most familiar with in all its various forms: plain (all-purpose), self-raising (self-rising), wholemeal, wheatgerm, and more. Wheat is sacred to the goddess Ceres and is linked with greater prosperity, fertility and abundance. It can also be used as a symbol for any magical wishes or intent: simply focus on your desires and knead those energies into the dough. It also signifies change and rebirth, from the old to the new. A lovely tradition is to bake a loaf of bread with a particular wish in mind, then cut a single slice and leave it out overnight (on your kitchen altar if you have one). In the morning, crumble the bread and throw it out for the birds, giving thanks for the abundance and blessings we have to share.

EGGS, DAIRY PRODUCTS, BUTTER & OILS

✸ BUTTER

Probably one of the most widely used baking ingredients, butter has been around for thousands of years and has always been seen as having both protective and prosperity energies. The faeries love it too, apparently, so it has some very magical qualities – ruled by the Moon, it brings about greater peace and tranquillity, particularly after arguments or discord. Apart from using it in baking, all sorts of herbs and spices can be added to butter to make even more magic blends.

✸ CHEESE

Another useful (and delicious) ingredient for baking, both sweet and savoury. Cheese is linked to the god Apollo and has long been linked to success, happiness and love. Use cheese liberally when preparing food for special occasions, because it brings with it lots of positive vibes for a happy outcome.

✸ EGGS

Such a simple thing, an egg – but possessed of such amazing qualities. Eggs have long been seen as symbols of the four elements – shell: earth; inner membrane: air; yolk: fire, and white: water. They are, understandably, a symbol of fertility, new growth and creativity. Use the freshest free-range/organic eggs for baking. Keep a bowl of fresh brown eggs in your kitchen, preferably in a small magic cauldron – they will keep negativity away and help your wishes come true.

✸ MILK

Dairy milk comes in so many forms: fresh, dried, condensed, evaporated – and from several different animals – but all milk carries with it feminine energies of nurturing and spirituality. Apart from baking it can also be used in lots of different ceremonies and rituals – try leaving a small cup of milk sweetened with a little honey in your kitchen overnight and you can expect a visit from the faeries! Bake recipes with milk at the time of the full moon, to honour the goddess within and above. Of course, if you are allergic to milk or prefer not to consume animal products, you can substitute non-dairy milks like oat, nut or soya.

✳ OLIVE OIL (AND OTHERS)

Olive oil possesses all the magical
attributes of olives: prosperity, fertility,
healing, peace and spirituality; olives have
been seen as sacred trees down through
the centuries. Extra virgin olive oil is
not generally recommended for baking,
because the strong and distinctive flavour
can come through, but light olive oil can
be used interchangeably with sunflower or
other vegetable oils in baking. Other oils
often used for baking include sunflower,
corn, safflower or canola oil; they all make
suitable oils for this purpose and are
generally fairly flavourless, so don't affect
the taste of the finished recipe.

OTHER MAGICAL INGREDIENTS & FLAVOURS

✳ CHOCOLATE

Starting with the Mayan and Aztec civilisations, chocolate has always been a powerful and magical food and flavouring – it's associated with the Heart chakra, which is probably why it works so well in offerings of love, including cakes, cookies, truffles, and more! On another note, chocolate is also suitable as an offering to the ancestors, so can be used in any rites related to this. Chocolate (and cocoa/unsweetened chocolate powder, its dried and ground form) raises and uplifts emotional energies and makes one feel positive and happy. Just sprinkling a little cocoa on a hot drink will bring about these warm and happy energies!

✳ COFFEE

Being half Italian, coffee is a subject very dear to my heart! It's been drunk since around 800 CE and has always been linked to energy, clarity of thought and achieving one's desires. It can also remove evil influences and change negative energies to positive ones. A little coffee can be added to most chocolate-flavoured baked goods as they work really well together. Add a few coffee beans to magical mixes and incense blends – this gives a lovely scent but also conjures a healthy dollop of protective magic.

✳ SALT

One of the most common ingredients we all know and use, but also one of the most powerful ones energetically and magically. Cleansing, purifying and protective, salt rids us and our homes of negative energies and harmful forces of all kinds. It's long been magical practice to sprinkle salt water in the corners of a room before rituals or any kind of cleansing. Full of feminine energies, salt is part of virtually all cooking and baking (in moderation, of course). Use it frugally, but with love, gratitude and awareness of its many gifts to us.

✳ TEA

Not just the usual black tea we are all familiar with, although that has plenty of magical properties of its own, but also green teas and herbal teas, all of which bring their own unique energies to our kitchen witchery. Tea leaves add a dash of strength and courage to our magical workings, and in the case of herbal teas also the extra physical and spiritual benefits of that particular herb. It's also nice to use tea (either black, green or herbal) as part of the liquid in a baking recipe – always well strained and cooled first, of course.

✳ VANILLA

Probably one of the most loved (and familiar) fragrances of the kitchen, vanilla is also a magical little bean, full of properties for love, passion, creativity and spirituality. Just burning a vanilla candle in your kitchen will lift you up to higher levels of happiness and consciousness.

✳ YEAST

Essential for bread and so many other baked goods, yeast has its own magical properties which include, not surprisingly, growth on both a personal and business level, and prosperity. Adding a little dried yeast to your purse or change jar is said to increase your financial abundance.

THE
RECIPES

SIMPLE AND GROUNDING

'There is beauty in simplicity.'
(Unknown)

As in so much of life, when we choose simplicity, things become clearer and more magical. This is true of cooking and baking too – often the simplest of recipes yield the most delicious results. This recipe section reminds us that we can choose simple enchantment ... in our kitchens and our lives.

LEKACH – SPICED HONEY BREAD

I love old cookbooks – the kind with spattered pages and lots of handwritten notes – they seem to hold a particular kind of kitchen magic, of memories and good times savoured and shared. I found this recipe some years ago in the back of just such an old cookbook, handwritten in green ink on a piece of faded paper. It just said – Lekach – a traditional honey bread from Eastern Europe. This is such a simple yet delicious recipe, equally good served at breakfast or for tea. And, of course, honey is one of the most magical foodstuffs out there!

SERVES 6-8

175 g (6 oz/½ cup) wildflower honey
125 g (4½ oz/½ cup) butter
100 g (3½ oz/½ cup) light brown sugar
30 ml (2 tablespoons) treacle
  (molasses)
30 ml (2 tablespoons) water
2 large eggs, beaten

250 g (9 oz/2 cups) self-raising flour
5 ml (1 teaspoon) ground
  cinnamon
2.5 ml (½ teaspoon) ground ginger
Finely grated zest of 1 orange
  (optional)

Preheat the oven to 180°C (350°F).

Grease a medium (23-cm/9-in) loaf or bread pan well.

Warm the honey, butter, sugar, treacle and water together in a large saucepan over gentle heat, until the butter has melted. Cool and then mix in the beaten eggs.

Sift together the flour and spices, and stir into the honey mixture to make a thick, smooth batter. Add the orange zest, if you are using it.

Bake for 40–50 minutes, or until the bread is well risen and shrinking a little from the sides of the tin. Cool briefly before turning the bread out onto a wire rack. This bread can be wrapped in foil and kept for 2–3 days before being served, as this allows the spice flavours to develop.

✹ WITCHY WISDOM

Honey is one of the most ancient and revered foodstuffs – a true gift from the bees and the Earth! Use it in recipes when you want to increase sweet harmony and communication in your home; add a few drops of honey to hot drinks for the same magic. If you need to have a difficult or painful conversation with someone, try placing a drop of honey on your tongue beforehand: it will make your words flow with greater ease and be received with an open heart.

CREAM TEA SWIRLS

Scones, in all their various permutations, are probably one of the simplest and most delicious forms of kitchen witchery: they use fairly basic ingredients and can usually be put together in well under an hour! And if you like the whole cream tea concept of scones, strawberry jam and cream these are even better, for they combine all of these in an easy to make - and eat! - package.

MAKES 12-15 SWIRLS

250 g (9 oz/2 cups) cake (superfine) flour
15 ml (3 teaspoons) baking powder
2.5 ml (½ teaspoon) salt
60 g (2 oz/¼ cup) unsalted butter
1 egg, large
250 ml (1 cup) buttermilk

For the filling:
250 ml (8 fl oz/1 cup) strawberry jam
    (preserve)

30 ml (2 tablespoons) fresh lemon juice
5 ml (1 teaspoon) chopped fresh thyme
    (optional)

For the glaze:
60 g (2 oz/½ cup) icing
    (powdered sugar)
2.5 ml (½ teaspoon) vanilla extract
65 ml (2 fl oz/¼ cup) single (light) cream

Preheat the oven to 200°C (400°F).

Line a large baking sheet with baking parchment, and grease lightly.

Make the filling by combining the jam, lemon juice and thyme (if using) in a small bowl, then set aside.

Sift the flour, baking powder and salt together in a large bowl; rub in the butter gently until the mixture resembles fine breadcrumbs. Beat the egg and buttermilk together in another bowl, then stir into the flour mixture to form a soft, but not sticky, dough. (You might need to add a little more buttermilk if the dough seems dry.)

On a floured board lightly press out the dough to form a rectangle measuring approximately 30 × 20 cm (12 × 8 in) and about 1 cm (½ in) thick. Carefully spread the jam mixture over the dough, leaving a 1-cm (½-in) border around the edges. Roll up from the long edge (like a Swiss roll) and press the edges together firmly. Use a long, sharp knife to cut the roll into slices, approximately 2.5 cm (1 in) thick.

Place the slices on the baking sheet, leaving a little space between them. Bake for 15–20 minutes, until the swirls are risen and golden brown. Make the glaze by mixing the icing sugar and vanilla extract with the cream until you have a spreadable consistency.

Cool the swirls on a wire rack and drizzle with the glaze. Add the filling once they are cold. They are best served fresh, on the day they are made.

✸ WITCHY WISDOM

Strawberries have such gentle heart wisdom; they are ideal fruits to include any time we need a little extra love and compassion, both for ourselves and others. Quite apart from using the fresh fruit on baked goods and desserts, it's also possible to make a simple strawberry syrup: combine 250 g (9 oz) of sliced strawberries in a small saucepan with 55 g (2 oz/¼ cup) of caster (superfine) sugar and 30 ml (2 tablespoons) of fresh lemon juice. Simmer gently until the strawberries are soft, then crush them slightly. (You can add water if the mixture is too dry.) Store in the fridge and drizzle over scones, plain sponge cake or chocolate mousse ... the choice is yours!

THE KITCHEN WITCH

OREGANO, BABY TOMATO & CHEDDAR CLAFOUTIS

Clafoutis is a traditional French dish, more often seen in a sweet incarnation, made with fruit such as fresh cherries, peaches, apples or figs. But this savoury version is also a delicious piece of kitchen magic, which can be served at breakfast, brunch or even as a light supper. It's not unlike a light quiche, but without the bother of making pastry! You can vary the herbs according to need or personal preference: basil and thyme both work well with the tomatoes and cheese.

SERVES 4-6

125g (4½ oz/1 cup) plain (all-purpose) flour
3 large eggs
250 ml (8 fl oz/1 cup) whole milk
15 ml (1 tablespoon) olive oil
250 g (9 oz) baby (cherry) tomatoes
65 g (2¼ oz/½ cup) finely grated Cheddar

30 ml (2 tablespoons) grated Parmesan
A small bunch of fresh oregano leaves, finely chopped
Salt and pepper, to taste

Preheat the oven to 180°C (350°F).

Grease a deep cake or tart tin (pan) (with a diameter of 25 cm/10 in) well with soft butter.

Prepare the batter by beating the flour, eggs, milk and olive oil together well, then add salt and pepper to taste. Remember cheese can be quite salty! Stir in the grated Cheddar and Parmesan.

Arrange the baby tomatoes evenly on the base of the cake/tart tin – cut them in half if they are quite large. Sprinkle the chopped oregano over them. Then pour the batter carefully over the herby tomatoes and bake for 25–30 minutes. The clafoutis should be set and golden brown. Serve hot or warm, cut into wedges – it makes a wonderful meal with good bread and a green salad with a sharp mustard dressing.

✴ WITCHY WISDOM

Eggs are, as we've already discussed, an extremely potent and life-affirming source of magic, but what to do with the empty shells? Try making cascarilla – an old enchanted mixture, traditionally used in Hoodoo and other ceremonies. Simply place clean, empty eggshells in a bag and crush them until they are quite fine. Mix the shell powder with fine sea salt and a little dried and crushed rosemary; sprinkle this mixture around the windowsills or entrance to your kitchen. It will banish negative, harmful forces and encourage peace and harmony in your living or cooking spaces.

THE KITCHEN WITCH

VANILLA & OLIVE OIL CAKE WITH ROSEMARY & LEMON SYRUP

This is such a simple, quick-to-put-together cake – I've been making versions of this since I was a child – but there is nothing simple about its powerful and healing energies! Lemons are, of course, one of the kitchen witch's favourite allies, with their purifying and uplifting qualities that are a gift from the Moon. Rosemary, too, is a strongly protective herb, used to ward off illness and negativity of all kinds. Make this cake for yourself or someone you love when you or they are feeling anxious and unable to make decisions or move forward in life. The recipe makes more rosemary syrup than you will need, but the leftovers can be stored in a small glass jar in the fridge for up to two weeks.

SERVES 8-10

250 g (9 oz/2 cups) plain (all-purpose) flour
2.5 ml (½ teaspoon) salt
12.5 ml (2½ teaspoons) baking powder
2 eggs, large
250 ml (8 fl oz/1 cup) plain Greek yoghurt (full-fat)
375 g (13 oz/1½ cups) caster (superfine) sugar
5 ml (1 teaspoon) vanilla extract

150 ml (5 fl oz/scant ⅔ cup) olive oil (don't use extra virgin olive oil, the taste is too strong – quite apart from the expense!: a more inexpensive or light olive oil is fine here)
Grated zest of 2 large lemons

For the syrup:
170 g (6 oz/¾ cup) caster (superfine) sugar
65 ml (2 fl oz/¼ cup) each fresh lemon juice and water
A few fresh rosemary sprigs

Preheat the oven to 170°C (340°F).

Grease a 23-cm (9-in) loaf pan well and line with baking parchment.

In a large bowl, sift together the flour, salt and baking powder. In another bowl beat together the eggs, yoghurt, sugar, vanilla extract, olive oil and lemon zest until well mixed. Pour into the flour mixture and gently beat together until you have a thick and smooth batter.

Pour into the prepared pan, and bake for 40–50 minutes, until the cake is risen and golden, and a thin skewer or similar inserted into it comes out clean. Cool for 10 minutes in the pan, then turn out onto a wire rack.

While the cake is cooking, make the syrup: combine the sugar, lemon juice and water in a small saucepan and heat gently until the sugar has dissolved. Add the rosemary sprigs to the hot syrup and allow to infuse for 5 minutes, then remove from the heat and strain the syrup. Prick the surface of the cake lightly with a fork, then spoon syrup over the top, allowing it to soak into the cake. Cool the cake completely and serve in slices; it will keep for a few days in an airtight container.

✳ WITCHY WISDOM

Always keep a few fresh lemons in your kitchen, for their protective and magical properties. According to legend, if you tie a lemon with red ribbons or thread and hang it up above the kitchen door, it will prevent any evil or harmful forces coming into the room.

LITTLE SAGE & CAMEMBERT FRITTERS

An ideal witchy snack to be served any time, but especially at celebratory feasts or springtime celebrations – cheese is a traditional food for this growing season. Sage is, of course, always a magical addition to foods, because this ancient herb carries such mystical powers of wisdom and insight. Just use it sparingly – it's also a strong herb that can become overpowering; unlike some herbs, it becomes stronger and more potent when dried.

MAKES 12-15 FRITTERS

125 g (4½ oz/1 cup) plain (all-purpose) flour
5 ml (1 teaspoon) salt
5 ml (1 teaspoon) dried sage, crumbled
2 eggs, separated

30 ml (2 tablespoons) melted butter
125 ml (4½ fl oz/½ cup) milk
125 g (4½ oz) Camembert cheese
Vegetable oil, for frying

Sift the flour, salt and dried sage together in a bowl. Make a well in the centre of the flour, and pour in two egg yolks, the melted butter and milk. Beat well to make a thick batter.

Remove the rind from the Camembert, and crumble the cheese into small pieces. Stir the cheese into the batter. Beat the egg whites until stiff but not dry, then fold them into the batter.

Heat a shallow (1-cm/½-in) layer of oil in a heavy-bottomed frying pan; fry generous tablespoonfuls of the batter mixture, turning once, until the fritters are golden brown and crisp around the edges.

Drain very well on some paper towel and serve warm.

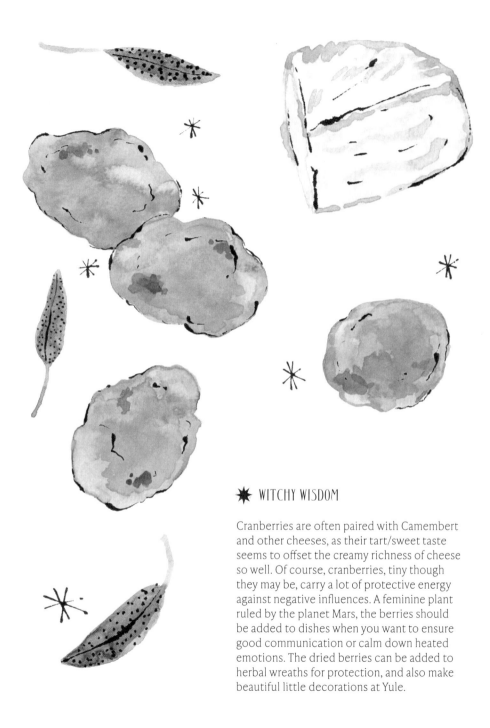

✳ WITCHY WISDOM

Cranberries are often paired with Camembert and other cheeses, as their tart/sweet taste seems to offset the creamy richness of cheese so well. Of course, cranberries, tiny though they may be, carry a lot of protective energy against negative influences. A feminine plant ruled by the planet Mars, the berries should be added to dishes when you want to ensure good communication or calm down heated emotions. The dried berries can be added to herbal wreaths for protection, and also make beautiful little decorations at Yule.

SPICED COFFEE LOAF

In the Middle East and North Africa strong black coffee is often warmed with the addition of spices such as coriander and cardamom, and that was the inspiration for this simple baked loaf, with an optional glaze. It's a brilliant morning pick-me-up and will bring extra clarity and inspiration to your day.

SERVES 10-12

---

5 ml (1 teaspoon) crushed cardamom seeds
5 ml (1 teaspoon) crushed coriander seeds
2 cloves (optional)
65 ml (2 fl oz/¼ cup) strong black coffee, hot
170 g (6 oz/¾ cup) unsalted butter, softened
170 g (6 oz/¾ cup) caster (superfine) sugar
2 eggs

250 g (9 oz/2 cups) plain (all-purpose) flour
7.5 ml (1½ teaspoons) baking powder
2.5 ml (½ teaspoon) bicarbonate of soda (baking soda)
2.5 ml (½ teaspoon) salt
250 ml (8 fl oz/1 cup) sour cream
125 g (4½ oz/1 cup) (powdered) sugar (optional)

Preheat the oven to 180°C (350°F).

Grease a large bread pan (or two smaller ones) well and line the base with baking parchment.

In a cup, combine the cardamom, coriander and cloves (if using) and pour the hot coffee over them. Set aside and allow to steep for 20–30 minutes.

Cream the butter and sugar together well, until light and fluffy, then gradually beat in the eggs. Sift the flour, baking powder, bicarbonate of soda and salt together in another bowl, then fold this mixture into the butter mixture, alternating with the sour cream. Lastly, stir in 30 ml (2 tablespoons) of the cooled coffee mixture. Spread the batter evenly in the prepared pan(s) and bake for 35–40 minutes, until the loaf is risen and a thin skewer or similar inserted into it comes out clean. Cool in the pan(s) for 10 minutes before turning out onto a wire rack to cool completely.

To make a coffee glaze (optional but delicious) combine the icing sugar in a small bowl with the remaining spiced coffee mixture. (Add a little water if the glaze seems too thick.) Pour the glaze over the loaf and allow it to set before serving.)

✸ WITCHY WISDOM

The spices used in this recipe, combined with the coffee, all have powerfully protective, warming and healing energies. Cardamom, in particular, stimulates body and mind, and is also known for increasing passion in a relationship! Add a few green cardamom pods to incense blends or magic mixes of any kind – they will bring greater love into your home.

THE KITCHEN WITCH

WALNUT CRUMBLE TEA CAKES

Tea cake is actually an old name for a little cookie – soft, buttery and delicious! But more than that, tea cakes make an excellent snack to serve at gatherings of all kinds, and can help us to become more grounded and focused after any kind of meditation or ritual work. Cookies have their own simple magic (flour, butter, sugar, eggs) but when we add specific herbs, spices or other ingredients they acquire those special energies, too.

MAKES ABOUT 15 COOKIES

For the walnut crumble:
65 g (2¼ oz/¼ cup) butter, softened
100 g (3½ oz/½ cup) light brown sugar
5 ml (1 teaspoon) ground cinnamon
60 g (2 oz/½ cup) finely chopped walnuts
30 ml (2 tablespoons) flour

For the tea cakes:
150 g (5½ oz/⅔ cup) butter, softened
2 egg yolks
175 g (6 oz/¾ cup) caster (superfine) sugar
2.5 ml (½ teaspoon) vanilla extract
185 g (4½ oz/1½ cups) cake (superfine) flour

Preheat the oven to 180°C (350°F).

Grease a large baking sheet well and line it with baking parchment.

Make the walnut crumble by creaming together the butter, brown sugar and cinnamon. Stir in the chopped walnuts and flour, to make a fine, crumbly mixture. Set aside.

To make the tea cakes, cream the butter very well with the egg yolks and sugar; stir in the vanilla extract, then sift over the flour and mix it in to make a smooth dough. Form the dough into balls the size of large walnuts and place them on the baking sheet. Use a teaspoon to create a shallow indentation in the top of each cookie, then fill this with a little of the walnut crumble. Bake the cookies until they are golden brown, about 15 minutes, then cool on a wire rack. They will keep in a tin for a couple of days, but seldom last that long!

In the very old cookbook where I found this recipe the original name was 'Wednesday Cookies' – interesting, in that the days of the week also have a lot of magical significance, with Wednesday being sacred to the Norse god Odin, who is linked to mysticism and creativity. Foods prepared on this day traditionally help us focus on our imaginative abilities and spirituality.

SUNDAY CAKE WITH SALTED CARAMEL SAUCE

The name of this cake reflects its relaxed simplicity – the perfect cake to share on a rainy Sunday afternoon, snuggled up indoors around a warm fire; yet it's also celebratory enough for dessert after a birthday dinner! The sauce is imbued with the subtle power and protective qualities of sea salt; however, this cake is infinitely versatile and can be served with a fruit coulis, or chocolate chips, chopped nuts or berries can be swirled into the batter.

SERVES 10-12

---

250 g (9 oz/2 cups) cake (superfine) flour
10 ml (2 teaspoons) baking powder
5 ml (1 teaspoon) salt
2.5 ml (½ teaspoon) ground cinnamon
170 g (6 oz/¾ cup) butter, softened
230 g (8 oz/1 cup) caster (superfine) sugar
100 g (3½ oz/½ cup) light brown sugar
3 large eggs
5 ml (1 teaspoon) vanilla extract

250 ml (8 fl oz/1 cup) buttermilk

For the sauce:
200 g (7 oz/1 cup) light brown sugar
125 ml (4½ fl oz/½ cup) single (light) cream
65 g (2¼ oz/¼ cup) butter
5 ml (1 teaspoon) vanilla extract
5 ml (1 teaspoon) fine sea salt flakes

Preheat the oven to 180°C (350°F).

Grease a deep 23-cm (9-in) square cake tin (pan) very well; there's a lot of batter in this recipe, and if the tin is too shallow it will overflow!

Sift the flour, baking powder, salt and cinnamon together in a medium bowl. In a large bowl cream the butter and two sugars together well, until the mixture is light and fluffy. Add the eggs, one at a time, and then the vanilla extract. Stir the dry ingredients into the butter mixture, alternating with the buttermilk until you have a smooth and creamy batter.

Pour the batter into the prepared tin and spread it out evenly. Bake for 30–35 minutes, or until the cake is well risen and golden brown, and a thin skewer or similar inserted into it comes out clean. Leave to cool in the pan for 15 minutes, then turn out onto a wire rack until it's cold.

To make the sauce, combine all the ingredients (apart from the salt) in a small, heavy-bottomed saucepan, and cook gently over a low heat, stirring all the time, until the sugar is dissolved and the butter melted. Remove from the heat and stir in the sea salt flakes. Serve the sauce warm, poured over squares of the cake.

★ WITCHY WISDOM

Although medical advice these days tells us to avoid too much salt, the truth is we do need some in our diets for our bodies to function at their best: as usual, moderation is the key. And always use pure, natural sea salt whenever possible – cheaper salts are often blended with less than natural ingredients! Unsurprisingly, this ancient and revered foodstuff is linked with many gods and goddesses, across all ages and cultures; the protective and healing qualities of salt have made it an indispensable part of kitchen and traditional magic.

NOURISH AND NATURE

'Cherish everything that makes you glad you are alive ...'

Hafiz

The foods we grow, prepare and eat are not only essential for maintaining physical life and well-being, but can also inspire and heal us on an emotional and spiritual level; this is one of the key beliefs and powers of kitchen witchery, as we learn to access, honour and celebrate the gifts of the Earth Mother in a simple and delicious way!

The recipes in this section are about baking with a view to nourishment and fulfilment for both body and mind, through the conscious choice of the ingredients we use, in particular herbs, spices, fruits and vegetables. Just a note: some people would say that baking is not necessarily a particularly healthful thing, but personally I believe the key is moderation, as always: eating what we love and enjoy but with awareness and restraint. Also, the foods we prepare and bake ourselves not only carry the personal energies of love and healing from our hands and heart, but are also made from natural ingredients, hopefully, with none of the strange chemical ingredients that are so often found in so-called convenience foods such as cake mixes and the like.

APPLE, VANILLA & THYME DESSERT CAKE

Most of us are probably fairly familiar with apple cake, but this one is a little different in that it contains no flour (thus making it suitable for those who are gluten intolerant); it's also warmed by the addition of thyme, a protective and invigorating herb that helps us to overcome pessimism and self-doubt, and find greater courage for facing everyday problems. Serve this cake with joy and hope to yourself or those you love when a fresh dose of inspiration is needed!

SERVES 1

---

4 large apples, peeled and cored
125 g (4½ oz/½ cup) soft butter
115 g (4 oz/½ cup) caster (superfine) sugar
80 g (2¾ oz/¾ cup) ground almonds
    (almond flour)

2 eggs
5 ml (1 teaspoon) vanilla extract
125 ml (4½ fl oz/½ cup) sour cream
15–30 ml (1–2 tablespoons) finely
    chopped fresh thyme leaves

Preheat the oven to 200°C (400°F).

Butter a medium ovenproof baking dish well.

Cut the apples into halves (or wedges) and arrange them in a single layer in the baking dish. Bake for 10–15 minutes, until they are slightly softened.

To make the batter, cream together the butter and sugar until the mixture is light and fluffy, then stir in the ground almonds. Add the eggs, one at a time. Stir in the vanilla extract and sour cream to make a smooth mixture. Take the apples out of the oven and spread the almond batter evenly over them. Sprinkle with the chopped thyme.

Bake for 15–20 minutes, until the batter is risen, set and golden. This dessert cake can be served warm or at room temperature, with single (light) cream. To create a delicious topping, warm 125 ml (4½ fl oz/½ cup) of apricot jam or preserve until runny, then stir in 15 ml (1 tablespoon) of brandy or rum. Brush this over the warm cake before serving.

✳ WITCHY WISDOM

Make an apple and herb simmer pot to add vibrant and positive energy to your kitchen space: fill a saucepan half-full with mineral or spring water, then add two small apples (not peeled, just cut into quarters or slices), a handful of fresh thyme leaves and a few cloves. Simmer gently until the bright, fresh aroma permeates the air; you can also add a few drops of thyme or lemon essential oil to this mixture.

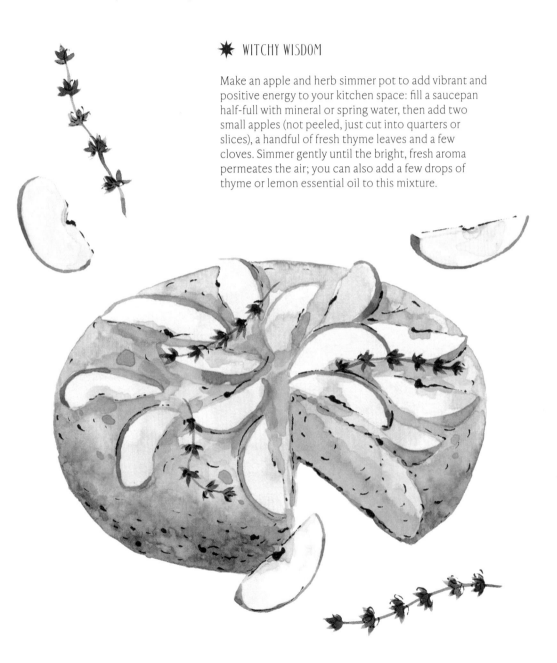

LEMON BALM RICE PUDDING

This dessert is based on Rizogalo, a traditional Greek rice pudding; the rose water might sound strange, but it really adds a delicate perfume to the dish and works well with the fresh taste of the lemon balm leaves. Just be sure to use culinary rose water. This is a truly magical pudding on so many levels: rice is one of the seven sacred grains that has sustained many generations across the globe, and it's a symbol of good fortune and protection (where the tradition of throwing rice at weddings originated). Lemon balm is one of the loveliest and most harmonising of herbs with its fresh citrus taste and aroma; it's particularly helpful when we are feeling anxious, depressed or frightened for whatever reason. I have served this dessert to people who are suffering the pain of grief and loss: it's a gentle reminder that healing will come, as it restores a sense of balance and peace.

SERVES 4-6

200 g (7 oz/1 cup) arborio rice (or similar short-grain rice)
750 ml (25 fl oz/3 cups) full cream milk
55 g (2 oz/¼ cup) caster (superfine) sugar
15 ml (1 tablespoon) culinary rose water
2.5 ml (½ teaspoon) vanilla extract
1 egg, separated

60 ml (2 fl oz/¼ cup) cream
Finely grated zest of a small lemon (optional)
A handful of fresh lemon balm leaves, roughly chopped or torn

Place the rice in a heavy-bottomed saucepan and add the milk and sugar. Cook over a very gentle heat, stirring frequently, until the rice is soft and the milk has been absorbed.

Stir in the rose water and vanilla extract; beat the egg yolk with the cream and add to the rice, together with the lemon zest, if you are using it, and stir well. Serve in a warmed ovenproof dish, scattered with the lemon balm leaves.

This pudding is also wonderful served cold: to do this, cool the rice mixture and then whip the egg white until stiff. Fold it gently into the rice, and then keep the pudding in the fridge until serving time.

✦ WITCHY WISDOM

Roses are not just one of nature's most beautiful icons, they are also incredibly healing for heartaches of all kinds, helping to calm and ease grief, anger, loneliness and sadness. A witch's kitchen should never be without a rose – I always have a fresh rose in a small jug on my kitchen altar, along with a rose-scented candle and a small bottle of rose essential oil; a few drops on a tissue or handkerchief will immediately lift your mood and make you feel tranquil and calm.

Rose ... may I learn from you how to love myself
in all my many moods and complexities,
and those around me with a clear and open heart.
In spirit and beauty, may it be so.

CINNAMON TEA CAKE WITH ALMOND GLAZE

Cinnamon is probably the most familiar kitchen spice for most of us, because it's used so widely, not only in baking but also in curries, sauces, chutneys and more. A simple cinnamon cake is much more powerful than it might seem at first glance for cinnamon punches above its weight in terms of both physical and emotional benefits; it's healing for the body when we are depleted and lacking in energy and generally acts as an overall mental and physical tonic. The almonds in this recipe also pack some powerful magic, in terms of increasing psychic powers, intuition and prosperity, while at the same time keeping negativity at bay.

SERVES 6-8

125 g (4½ oz/½ cup) unsalted butter
185 g (6½ oz/1½ cups) plain (all-purpose) flour
55 g (2 oz/½ cup) ground almonds (almond flour)
185 g (6½ oz/1 cup) soft brown sugar
10 ml (2 teaspoons) baking powder
2.5 ml (½ teaspoon) salt
15 ml (1 tablespoon) ground cinnamon

2 eggs
125 ml (4½ fl oz/½ cup) buttermilk
5 ml (1 teaspoon) vanilla extract

For the glaze:
65 g (2¼ oz/¼ cup) butter
90 g (3¼ oz/¾ cup) icing (powdered) sugar
10 ml (2 teaspoons) vanilla extract
100 g (3½ oz/½ cup) slivered almonds

Preheat the oven to 180°C (350°F).

Grease a 23-cm (9-in) cake tin (pan) or cast-iron skillet very well.

Melt the unsalted butter in a small saucepan until golden, then remove from the heat and allow to cool. In a large bowl sift together the flour, ground almonds, brown sugar, baking powder, salt and cinnamon. In another small bowl beat together the eggs, buttermilk, vanilla extract and melted butter, then add this to the flour mixture and beat well. Pour into the tin and bake for 10-15 minutes.

While the cake is baking, prepare the glaze by melting the butter together with the icing sugar and vanilla extract until the mixture is thick and creamy. Stir in the slivered almonds and remove from the heat. Take the cake out of the oven and spread the glaze evenly over the top, then return to the oven and bake for a further 15-20 minutes. This cake can be served warm or at room temperature.

✳ WITCHY WISDOM

Cinnamon sugar is a wonderful addition to the kitchen witch's pantry and is easily made by placing a few cinnamon sticks in a jar of granulated or brown sugar; seal the jar and leave in a dry place for a couple of weeks before removing the sticks. You can, of course, simply stir a little ground cinnamon into the sugar but somehow that loses some of the magical impact! This sugar is great sprinkled over pancakes, scones, cookies, porridge, and so on. To ensure your kitchen (and home) are well protected and open to good fortune, gather together a few cinnamon sticks, a couple of dried bay leaves and a few stems of rosemary, tie them with a red or gold ribbon, and hang them over your kitchen or front door.

GLUTEN-FREE CARROT, APPLE & SPICE MUFFINS

Both carrots and apples were once considered to be powerful ingredients in love potions – perhaps that's not surprising, given that the masculine energies of the carrot work in harmony with the feminine power of the apple, one of the most ancient and magical fruits of all. These simple muffins make a good portable breakfast or snack and can help to imbue us with greater clarity and awareness, both of ourselves and the world around us. Apples, in particular, are also linked with the afterlife and spirit world, so can be used as a gentle reminder of our ancestors and the links between past, present and future.

MAKES 6 LARGE OR 12 SMALL MUFFINS

---

80 g (2¾ oz/¾ cup) ground almonds (almond flour)
60 g (2 oz/½ cup) fine semolina
30 g (1 oz/¼ cup) cornflour (cornstarch)
10 ml (2 teaspoons) baking powder
5 ml (1 teaspoon) each ground cinnamon and ginger
2.5ml (½ teaspoon) each nutmeg and ground coriander

2 eggs
200 g (7 oz/1 cup) light brown sugar
125 ml (4½ fl oz/½ cup) vegetable or coconut oil
350 g (12 oz/1¾ cups) finely grated carrots
1 large apple, peeled and finely grated
Zest of 1 orange
60 g (2 oz/½ cup) finely chopped pecans (optional)

Preheat the oven to 180°C (350°F).

Line a 6-hole or 12-hole muffin tin (pan) with paper liners.

In a large bowl stir together the ground almonds, semolina, cornflour, baking powder and ground spices. In another bowl beat the eggs, brown sugar and oil to make a thick, smooth batter. Stir the liquid mixture into the dry one and beat quickly to combine – don't overmix. Lastly, add the carrots, apple and pecans (if using).

NOURISH AND NATURE

Distribute the batter evenly between the prepared muffin holes, filling them about two-thirds full. Bake for 20 minutes, or until the muffins are well risen and golden brown.

Create a delicious topping by combining 65 ml (2 fl oz/½ cup) light brown sugar with 5 ml (1 teaspoon) of ground cinnamon and 2.5 ml (½ teaspoon) of ground ginger; sprinkle a little of this on top of each muffin before baking.

Should you not require a gluten-free option, the ground almonds can be omitted and replaced by cake (superfine) flour.

✳ WITCHY WISDOM

The chakras (the word comes from the Sanskrit and means vortex) are the seven energy centres that link both the physical body and spirit/emotions. Carrots, with their vibrant orange colour, are linked to the second chakra, the Sacral chakra, which is situated just below the navel. When we are in healthy balance in this chakra, we are joyful and creative, and live our lives to their fullest purpose.

CHAI TORTE WITH GINGER CREAM

Though I've known (and loved) the spicy magic of chai tea for some time, I had honestly never thought of using it in baking until I read Melissa Forti's amazing book, *The Italian Baker*; apart from our common Italian heritage, she's clearly a true kitchen witch! This recipe is adapted from one in her book, but I have simplified it somewhat. Chai Masala (the words mean 'spiced tea' in Hindi) is becoming increasingly popular all over the world, and not surprisingly, for the ingredients of this magical brew include (but are not limited to) ginger, cardamom, cinnamon, cloves, star anise and black pepper. All of these warming spices boost our metabolism and mood on every level. Chai tea supports good digestive function and circulation and serves as a great tonic when we are feeling exhausted, ungrounded or generally depleted, particularly in the cooler months. If you prefer not to use dairy, it's perfectly fine to use oat, soy, coconut or nut milks. You can also whip up chilled coconut cream and use that in the topping.

SERVES 6-8

125 ml (4½ fl oz/½ cup) milk
4 chai tea bags
125 g (4½ oz/½ cup) unsalted butter, softened
250 g (9 oz/1 cup) granulated sugar
2 large eggs
5 ml (1 teaspoon) vanilla extract
185 g (6½ oz/1½ cups) plain (all-purpose) flour
10 ml (2 teaspoons) baking powder
2.5 ml (½ teaspoon) salt
5 ml (1 teaspoon) ground cinnamon
2.5 ml (½ teaspoon) ground cardamom

For the ginger cream:
225 g (8 oz) full fat cream cheese, at room temperature
65 g (2¼ oz/¼ cup) butter, softened
5 ml (1 teaspoon) vanilla extract
125 g (4½ oz/1 cup) icing (powdered) sugar
30 ml (2 tablespoons) crystallised ginger, finely chopped

Preheat the oven to 180°C (350°F).

Grease a 23-cm (9-in) cake tin (pan) well and line the base with baking parchment.

Warm the milk gently in a small saucepan, then add the tea bags. Remove from the heat and allow the mixture to infuse for at least 10 minutes. Discard the tea bags and allow the milk to cool.

In a large bowl, cream the butter and sugar together until the mixture is light and fluffy. Add the eggs, one at a time, and then the vanilla extract. Sift the dry ingredients together in a separate bowl and then add to the butter mixture, alternating the dry ingredients and cooled milk.

Spread the batter evenly in the prepared cake tin, and bake for 30–40 minutes, or until a thin skewer or similar inserted into the cake comes out clean. Cool in the tin for 10 minutes before turning out onto a wire rack to cool completely.

To make the topping, mix the cream cheese and butter together until smooth, then stir in the vanilla extract and sugar to make a creamy mixture. If it's too soft, place in the fridge for a while to firm up. Swirl the creamy cheese topping over the cake and sprinkle with the chopped ginger.

✴ WITCHY WISDOM

Ginger is another very powerful spice on many levels and can be used to increase psychic and magical awareness. Not only good for baking and cooking, a little powdered ginger can also be added to incense or sprinkling mixtures and simmer pots, and will help keep potentially harmful forces at bay, while at the same time increasing success and prosperity. Infuse some freshly sliced ginger in a little jar of sweet almond oil and use this oil in magical rituals of all kinds.

CARDAMOM & HONEY COOKIES

The greatest magic lies in simplicity, and these easy-to-make cookies certainly prove this timeless truth! As for their ingredients, well, honey is sweet, golden magic in a jar, a magic which is augmented by the use of herbs and spices. These simple, crisp cookies are warmed with cardamom, one of the most ancient spices much used in North African and Middle Eastern cooking. It's a good spice to choose when we are looking to increase happiness and joy in our lives, and maybe add some renewed passion – especially if we are feeling flat and jaded in our relationships, or in ourselves. These simple cookies are also a nice introduction to magical baking for children – although some might find the cardamom a bit unusual! It's perfectly fine to use cinnamon or ginger instead, in that case. Kitchen witches are flexible and know that nothing is written in stone!

MAKES 10-50 COOKIES

125 g (4½ oz/½ cup) unsalted butter
115 g (4 oz/½ cup) caster (superfine) sugar
65 ml (2 fl oz/¼ cup) organic honey
5 ml (1 teaspoon) vanilla extract
65 ml (2 fl oz/¼ cup) water

250 g (9 oz/2 cups) plain (all-purpose) flour
2.5 ml (½ teaspoon) bicarbonate of soda
   (baking soda)
10 ml (2 teaspoons) ground cardamom
5 ml (1 teaspoon) ground ginger (optional)

(This recipe has to be started the day before, as ideally the dough must rest in the fridge for at least 12 hours/overnight.)

Line two large baking trays (pans) with baking parchment.

In a medium saucepan melt the butter gently, then add the sugar, honey, vanilla extract and water. Stir gently until the sugar has dissolved and the mixture is smooth. Remove from the heat.

Sift together the dry ingredients, then pour them into the butter mixture and mix together with a wooden spoon – the dough will be a bit crumbly.

NOURISH AND NATURE

Knead the dough lightly on a floured wooden board until it comes together, then divide it into two. Shape into two round logs, about 6 cm (2½ in) wide. Wrap each log in baking parchment or cling film (plastic wrap), and chill for at least 12 hours.

The next day preheat the oven to 180°C (350°F).

Unwrap the logs and use a very sharp knife to cut the dough into thin slices (no more than 5 mm/¼ in). Arrange on the baking trays and bake for 8–10 minutes, until the cookies are crisp and golden. Allow to cool on the baking trays. These cookies keep well in an airtight tin.

✳ WITCHY WISDOM

A few crushed/broken cardamom seeds can be added to many recipes for food and drink; they also work magically on a powerful level, bringing greater protection, love and affection into the home. Add a few whole cardamom seeds to any cleansing or protective mixture, or make tiny 'free from harm' bags by mixing a few dried bay leaves, a handful of rice grains and a couple of cardamom seeds in small fabric bags. Carry one of these with you or give them to your loved ones when they are out and about or going on a journey.

THE KITCHEN WITCH

LEMON & LAVENDER CAKE

The familiar sweet and flowery fragrance of lavender is underlined with a surprising strength; it's probably one of the most-loved herbs of all, yet often less used in cooking than it deserves to be – in moderation, otherwise the taste can overwhelm all else! Apart from its many health benefits, which include helping ease headaches, muscle strain, sleeplessness, exhaustion and general physical depletion, lavender also gently lifts and soothes the spirit, calming anxiety and bringing a renewed sense of peace and well-being. This cake is perfect for a quiet afternoon of reflection and mindfulness. I love this quote by Brittany Wood Nickerson:

'Lavender lessons are life lessons:
to enjoy, to accept, to love and to let go.'

SERVES 8-10

185 g (6½ oz/1½ cups) plain (all-purpose) flour
2.5 ml (½ teaspoon) salt
10 ml (2 teaspoons) baking powder
30 ml (2 tablespoons) dried lavender leaves/ blossoms, crumbled
2 eggs
15 ml (1 tablespoon) finely grated lemon zest
250 ml (8 fl oz/1 cup) buttermilk

285 g (10 oz/1¼ cups) caster (superfine) sugar
5 ml (1 teaspoon) vanilla extract
165 ml (5½ fl oz/⅔ cup) vegetable oil

For the syrup:
115 g (4 oz/½ cup) caster (superfine) sugar
125 ml (4½ fl oz/½ cup) fresh lemon juice
Extra dried lavender blossoms (optional)

Preheat the oven to 180°C (350°F).

Grease a medium loaf/bread pan well and line the base with baking parchment.

In a large bowl sift together the flour, salt, baking powder and dried lavender. In another bowl beat the eggs, lemon zest, buttermilk, sugar, vanilla extract and oil until well blended, then gently stir this into the flour mixture and beat to combine. Pour the batter into the prepared pan and bake for 35–40 minutes, or until the loaf is well-risen and a thin skewer or similar inserted into it comes out clean.

In the meantime, make the syrup by mixing the sugar and lemon juice together until the sugar has dissolved. When the loaf comes out of the oven, cool briefly, then turn it out onto a wire rack. Prick the surface of the cake all over with a fork, then gently spoon over the lemon syrup, allowing it to soak into the cake. Sprinkle with a little extra crushed lavender, if you like.

✹ WITCHY WISDOM

Lemons, the other taste element in this cake, are intrinsically linked to the Moon, and carry all the spiritual and magical female energies of this most mysterious celestial body. Bake this cake on a Monday (Moon Day), preferably at night when the kitchen is quiet and still, enhancing the magic. Allow yourself to dream and envision whatever changes you want to make in your life: family, love, work or anything else. (You might also choose to write in your journal about this.) Keep your thoughts clear and positive as you light a single white candle and enjoy a slice of this cake while knowing that new joy and energy will soon fill you, like the clear silver light of the Moon.

Moon Goddess, hear and empower me
with inspiration, vision and understanding
as you bless me with your enchanted light.
Thank you ... so may it be.

BAKING
SEASONAL MAGIC

'Nature does not hurry,
yet everything is accomplished ...'

Lao Tzu

The natural wheel of the year, with its changing seasons and magical energies, is obviously of great significance to green and kitchen witches, and this has been the case since ancient times. In those days, people lived close to the land, tied closely to the Earth's seasonal bounty – but even though that may not be so much the case now, we can still choose to follow the natural rhythms and cycles of the year to create greater magic, well-being and joy.

For this section I have chosen the eight sabbats of the Wheel of the Year – these are generally the lunar and solar solstices/equinoxes and the points in between – each of these sabbats has its own traditions, rituals and magical food correspondences, and here you will find a simple recipe for each sabbat, together with other ideas for making it magical!

MORGANA'S CHOCOLATE TARTS

Samhain on 31 October – now largely known as Halloween – is the traditional start of the year, and also probably the most magical of all the holidays in the seasonal cycle, despite its commercialisation! So it seems appropriate to include a recipe that honours Morgana, a dark goddess, linked to the Arthurian legend, who is especially honoured at Samhain – a time of drawing together the dark and light sides of human nature, as well as a powerful time for connecting to the world of spirits and those who have gone before us. These chocolate tarts filled with a bittersweet ganache are a perfect reflection of this sacred time, especially as chocolate is related to offerings for the ancestors and spirits. You can make a large tart or several smaller ones from the recipe, but I prefer to make quite a few tiny ones (using a mini muffin tin/pan or tartlet tins) as the filling is so rich. You can also use the crisp and buttery pastry to make Samhain cookies as a friend of mine does – she's especially fond of making little cats, owls and stars!

MAKES 1 LARGE, 6 SMALL OR UP TO 18 MINI TARTS

For the pastry:
125 g (4½ oz/½ cup) butter, softened
40 g (1½ oz/⅓ cup) icing (powdered) sugar
2.5 ml (½ teaspoon) salt
1 egg
5 ml (1 teaspoon) vanilla extract
250 g (9 oz/2 cups) plain (all-purpose) flour
30 g (1 oz/¼ cup) (unsweetened chocolate)
    cocoa powder

For the filling:
250 ml (8 fl oz/1 cup) single (light) cream
5 ml (1 teaspoon) crushed cardamom seeds
    (optional)
250 g (9 oz) good-quality dark chocolate
Cherries

Preheat the oven to 160°C (325°F).

Grease the muffin tin (pan) or tartlet tins (of your chosen size) well.

Cream the butter and sugar together, then add the salt, egg and vanilla extract. Stir in the flour and cocoa to make a soft but manageable dough. Roll the pastry out on a board to a thickness of no more than 5 mm (¼ in), then line your chosen tins with the pastry, and prick the base of the pastry lightly with a fork. Bake for 10–15 minutes, then cool in the tins before removing the pastry cases and transferring carefully to a wire rack.

Make the ganache filling by warming the cream gently in a small saucepan until it's hot, but not boiling. Add the crushed cardamom seeds if you are using them. Break the chocolate into small pieces in a bowl, then pour over half the warm cream, stirring well until the chocolate has melted. Then add the rest of the cream: the mixture should be thick and smooth.

Divide the ganache evenly between the cooled pastry cases, then chill the tarts for a couple of hours, until the filling has set. Remove from the fridge 30 minutes before serving; top each tart with a dark cherry.

✷ WITCHY WISDOM

Rosemary is a traditional herb for this time of year, with its links to remembrance and the ancestors; we all need to remember and acknowledge who we are and where we came from, and there is no better time than Samhain to do this. It's also a particularly good time for writing in our kitchen grimoire or journal, as we reflect on our lives and what has led us to this point in time. Many people choose this time of year to honour those who have gone before in a very practical way, by making and sharing recipes they loved or enjoyed; I have done this for both my parents and it's always a meaningful (if somewhat bittersweet) ritual. I like to place a few sprigs of fresh rosemary in a little blue glass vase on my kitchen altar, next to small pictures of my mother and great aunt (who taught me to bake); it's also nice to say a short blessing:

I remember you with love, with sweet memories.
You are still part of me, part of my life,
and always will be.
Nothing truly loved can be lost –
that is the wonder and magic of this Earth.
Blessed be. And so it is.

SNOWY NIGHT PUDDING

Yule, which traditionally occurs on or near the Winter Solstice (21 December), is obviously much overshadowed by Christmas these days, but should be honoured and celebrated in its own right. Strangely, although it marks the official beginning of winter, it is also the time when the days begin to grow longer again, and in many cultures was celebrated as the return of the light. In the deep, dark days of winter we need to be reminded that growth continues, both in and around us: the cold ground holds the magic of seeds that will bloom again in their own time and the longest night will give way to light. This dark and aromatic pudding is a delicious reminder of these truths, and is laden with the fruits of the earth; it's actually a very old recipe, handed down from my great-grandmother – I never knew her – but she was Scottish and apparently a kitchen witch of some note!

SERVES 6

250 g (9 oz) finely chopped pitted dates
125 g (4½ oz/½ cup) butter
5 ml (1 teaspoon) bicarbonate of soda
    (baking soda)
250 ml (8 fl oz/1 cup) boiling water
185 g (6½ oz/1½ cups) cake (superfine) flour
5 ml (1 teaspoon) baking powder
5 ml (1 teaspoon) each ground cinnamon
    and ground ginger
2 eggs
5 ml (1 teaspoon) vanilla extract
95 g (3½ oz/½ cup) soft brown sugar

65 ml (2 fl oz/¼ cup) dark treacle (molasses)
60 g (2 oz/½ cup) chopped walnuts or pecans
    (optional)
60 g (2 oz/½ cup) raisins

For the sauce:
65 g (2¼ oz/¼ cup) butter
115 g (4 oz/½ cup) caster (superfine) sugar
125 ml (4½ fl oz/½ cup) single (light) cream
65 ml (2 fl oz/3 tablespoons) whisky or
    Southern Comfort

🌿 BAKING SEASONAL MAGIC

Preheat the oven to 160°C (325°F).

Grease a medium-sized oval or square baking dish very well.

Place the dates, butter and bicarbonate of soda in an ovenproof glass bowl; pour over the boiling water and leave to stand until the butter has melted.

Sift the flour, baking powder and spices together. In a large bowl beat the eggs, vanilla extract, sugar and treacle together until smooth. Stir the cooled date mixture into the eggs, then gradually add the flour in increments, beating well to make a thick batter. Finally, stir in the nuts (if using) and raisins. Pour the batter into the prepared baking dish and bake for 30 minutes, until the pudding has risen.

While the pudding is baking, prepare the sauce by heating the butter, sugar and cream together gently until the sugar has dissolved and the sauce is smooth. Stir in the whisky (you can also use fresh orange juice if you prefer not to add alcohol). Take the pudding out of the oven and spoon the sauce evenly over the surface, before returning it to the oven for another 10 minutes. Serve warm, with dollops of whipped cream (or scoops of vanilla ice cream) to carry on the 'snowy' theme!

✳ WITCHY WISDOM

Embrace the inner warmth and fire of this season by burning red and green candles in your kitchen: red reflects the colour of the returning Sun, and green symbolises new life. Incense, too, or scented candles add a festive and spiritual note; try pine, frankincense, cedarwood, juniper or spicy scents like cinnamon or nutmeg. Wassail cup is a traditional drink for Yule night, and can be made with alcohol or not, as you prefer. Gently simmer 1 bottle of red wine (or apple cider/juice) with 115 g (4 oz/½ cup) of sugar, the zest and juice of one orange, cinnamon sticks and a few cloves; when the sugar has dissolved, strain into small cups and drink warm, sharing thoughts and wishes for this season of hope and magic!

SPRING HERB PANCAKES WITH CREAMY SAUCE

Imbolc, which takes place around 2 February, is a traditional Celtic festival, marking the very beginning of spring, of warmth and new growth. It's also dedicated to the Irish fire goddess Brigid, who is the keeper of fire, so very important to us kitchen witches, then! Light dishes such as pancakes and omelettes are traditionally associated with this time of year; include dairy products and lots of fresh herbs in your baking for this season. Dairy products (and eggs) are considered sacred to spring/Imbolc, and of course fresh herbs echo the green freshness of the new season. It's also an ideal time to plant seeds (even in a kitchen window box) so that you can enjoy the miracle of new life unfolding.

MAKES 10-12 SMALL PANCAKES

125 g (4½ oz/1 cup) cake (superfine) flour
10 ml (2 teaspoons) baking powder
2.5 ml (½ teaspoon) salt
Pinch each of black pepper and ground coriander
A handful of fresh chives, finely snipped (garlic chives are great, too)
15 ml (1 tablespoon) chopped fresh dill
60 g (2 oz/1 cup) baby spinach leaves, finely shredded
2 eggs, separated
250 ml (8 fl oz/1 cup) buttermilk
30 ml (2 tablespoons) melted butter
Oil/butter, for frying

For the sauce:
250 ml (8 fl oz/1 cup) thick Greek yoghurt
45 ml (3 tablespoons) olive oil
30 ml (2 tablespoons) crème fraiche or sour cream
Zest of a small lemon
5 ml (1 teaspoon) Dijon mustard
A small handful of finely chopped fresh herbs, such as thyme, chives or coriander
Salt and pepper, to taste

Sift the flour, baking powder, salt and ground pepper/coriander together in a bowl. Stir in the chopped fresh herbs and spinach. In a small bowl beat together the egg yolks, buttermilk and melted butter, then stir this into the flour mixture until combined. Beat the egg whites until stiff but not dry and fold them gently into the batter.

Heat a heavy skillet/frying pan with a little butter or oil over a medium-high heat. Pour about 65 ml (2 fl oz/¼ cup) of batter into the pan at a time and cook until small and golden bubbles appear on the surface of the pancake. Flip over and cook for another 2 minutes. You can cook a few pancakes at a time, but don't crowd the pan!

Keep the little pancakes warm until serving time; they can be served plain with butter but are particularly delicious when filled with feta cheese and pickles and served with a little spicy chutney or a dollop of creamy herb sauce (see recipe below).

To make the sauce, mix all the ingredients (apart from the herbs) together well in a small bowl. Stir in the herbs and keep in the fridge before serving.

NOTE: These little pancakes can be made with any of your favourite herbs – I just happen to love chives and dill! The spinach adds a fresh green note but can be omitted if you prefer.

✳ WITCHY WISDOM

We are all familiar with the concept of spring cleaning, which was traditionally done at this time of year. It was a case of 'out with the old, in with the new', which is entirely in keeping with the magic of spring. We can also do a spring clean of our hearts and spirits, using some simple kitchen magic. Simmer some water in a small pot and add a few drops of lavender and rosemary essential oil, and a few dried sage leaves; breathe in the beautiful fragrance and allow it to fill you with fresh hope and inspiration. Let go of regret for times past and things done – it's the time for fresh and hopeful beginnings. So, try to do something new on this day – even if it's as simple as experimenting with a different recipe or ingredient you haven't used before.

RHUBARB KUCHEN

Ostara – which occurs around 21 March (the date varies from year to year) – is the Spring Equinox, when day and night are of equal length. This is a festival for finding balance and casting off that which no longer serves us well. It's a time of magic and new hope; who among us doesn't feel a sense of joy with the coming of the first days of spring, with bright blossoms and the tender green shoots of leaves on winter-bare trees? Ostara was also linked to fertility – of the Earth in general, as well as that of human beings and animals; it was considered the time of birth and beginnings. Eggs were particularly symbolic at this time, which is probably the origin of the tradition of Easter eggs, too. This *kuchen* recipe is particularly suitable for this time of year, because it includes fresh spring rhubarb, eggs and cream; however, this is a simplified version of traditional *kuchen*, which is usually made with yeast. Please note that it can also be made with other fruit such as apples, peaches and figs.

SERVES 6-8

---

175 g (6 oz) fresh young rhubarb
55 g (2 oz/¼ cup) caster (superfine) sugar
1 star anise pod
A few cardamom seeds

For the topping:
125 ml (4½ fl oz/½ cup) single (light) cream
115 g (4 oz/½ cup) caster (superfine) sugar
1 egg
30 ml (2 tablespoons) plain (all-purpose) flour

For the cake:
185 g (6½ oz/1½ cups) plain (all-purpose) flour
10 ml (2 teaspoons) baking powder
2.5 ml (½ teaspoon) salt
3 eggs
115 g (4 oz/½ cup) caster (superfine) sugar
5 ml (1 teaspoon) vanilla extract
125 g (4½ oz/½ cup) butter, melted and cooled
Finely grated zest of a small lemon (optional)

Grease a 23-cm (9-in) round springform cake tin (pan) well and dust with a little flour.

Prepare the rhubarb before heating the oven: cut the rhubarb stalks into pieces no larger than 1.5 cm (½ in) and place in a saucepan together with the sugar, star anise and cardamom seeds. Cover with water and simmer gently for around 10 minutes until the sugar has dissolved, and the rhubarb is just tender – not mushy! Drain the fruit and allow it to cool completely.

Preheat the oven to 190°C (375°F).

Sift the flour, baking powder and salt together. In another bowl, beat the eggs, sugar and vanilla extract very well until the mixture is thick and pale, then stir in the melted butter. Lastly, gently fold in the flour mixture.

Pour the batter into the prepared cake tin. Arrange the cooled rhubarb evenly over the surface of the cake.

Beat the ingredients for the topping together well, then spoon over the rhubarb and spread the topping out evenly. Bake for 25–30 minutes, until the topping has set and is pale golden brown. Allow to cool in the tin for a few minutes, then loosen the sides and base of the tin and lift the cake out onto a wire rack. This *kuchen* is at its best served fresh and still a little warm.

✴ WITCHY WISDOM

Decorate your kitchen with spring blooms – particularly daffodils, which have such a beautiful and gentle energy. And creating a basket of mantra eggs (painted eggs featuring a hopeful word) is a lovely way of spending time with friends and family. Make holes with a large needle or small nail in each end of the egg, then hold the egg over a bowl and blow through one hole so the contents come out the other end. This can be a slow process – a friend of mine bribes her children to do it for her (the reward being a chocolate egg!); keep the liquid eggs for baking and then gently rinse the empty shells inside and out. Dry thoroughly before painting with acrylic paints, either plain or with patterns and pictures. We've had a lot of magical fun writing messages and mantras on the eggs with waterproof pens – even words like 'Dream', 'Grace', 'Believe' ... pile the eggs in a basket on your kitchen table and let people choose one that represents the message of spring for them.

CROSTOLI

Beltane is the early summer festival of the Wheel of the Year and happens on 1 May. It's a time of celebration and abundance, a time to honour all living and growing things (including ourselves). Many significant life ceremonies such as weddings and handfastings are planned for this time. A handfasting is a traditional pagan/Wiccan marriage ceremony, often held outside and accompanied by much feasting and joy! Handfastings are once again becoming increasingly popular as a marriage/commitment celebration. But Beltane can also simply be a happy way to enjoy the company of family and friends. If the weather permits, cook and eat outdoors – simple and easy meals accompanied by lots of laughter are the gifts of Beltane. These traditional Italian fried treats are the perfect snack to enjoy at this time; I grew up making variations of this recipe, and they always disappeared very quickly, so it might be wise to make a double batch!

MAKES ABOUT 25 CROSTOLI (WHICH ARE NEVER ENOUGH!)

---

500 g (1 lb 2 oz/4 cups) plain (all-purpose) flour
10 ml (2 teaspoons) baking powder
2 eggs, beaten
65 g (2¼ oz/¼ cup) soft butter

55 g (2 oz/¼ cup) caster (superfine) sugar
125 ml (4½ fl oz/½ cup) white wine
Vegetable oil, for deep frying
Icing (powdered) sugar, for dusting

Sift the flour and baking powder into a large bowl, then add the eggs, butter and sugar until the mixture comes together. Stir in the wine to make a soft, slightly sticky dough – depending on the flour used, you might need to add more liquid or flour.

Roll the dough out on a floured board; it must be very thin, no more than 2–3mm (⅛ in) thick. Cut the dough into strips 3 cm (1¼ in) wide by 10 cm (4 in) long – I like to use a ravioli cutter, which makes a pretty fluted edge. Gently press each strip together in the middle, so it forms a small bow shape.

Heat oil in a deep frying pan; test the heat by dropping in one pastry. It should cook and brown in 10–15 seconds. Cook a few crostoli at a time, turning them once so they are crisp and golden on both sides. Remove with a spatula and drain very well on some paper towels. Dust liberally with icing sugar before serving.

You can also make a magical dessert platter by placing the crostoli in the centre of a round tray and surrounding them with a few bowls of sweet dipping sauces, such as caramel, chocolate and strawberry.

✴ WITCHY WISDOM

The bright energy of Beltane is the perfect time to make wishes – this is also a lovely group activity to be done in the garden or other green space. Everyone takes a few small pieces of paper, cut into label shapes, and writes down a few wishes – punch holes in the top of the labels and thread with colourful ribbons or lengths of wool. Tie the labels onto the branches of a tree (or use a discarded tree branch planted in a pot); gather round and say the following:

Wishes here for all to see,
wishes from my heart and soul.
Bright summer magic,
grant my wishes one and all.
And so it is.

You can leave the labels tied to the tree if it is appropriate to do so, otherwise place them on your kitchen altar.

ROSE & PASSION FRUIT DROPS

Litha is the Summer Solstice on 21 June and marks the point at which days shorten and nights lengthen, as the Earth turns towards winter. However, this is the time to celebrate the gifts of the Earth – particularly her flowers and fruits – and to remind ourselves of the inner light we all carry. Sometimes we lose confidence in ourselves and our abilities to make a difference in the world, but at this time we can draw on summer's energy to help us create the lives we want and need. The recipe here contains both roses and passion fruit (from the passion flower vine); these flowers are great for creating and enhancing self-esteem and inner beauty. Serve the cookies with feelings of joy and hope – and perhaps cups of delicate rose and jasmine tea?

MAKES ABOUT 15-20 COOKIES

125 g (4½ oz/½ cup) unsalted butter,
    softened
60 g (2 oz/½ cup) icing (powdered) sugar
2.5 ml (½ teaspoon) vanilla extract
10 ml (2 teaspoons) culinary rose water
15 ml (1 tablespoon) passion fruit pulp
2 egg whites

55 g (2 oz/½ cup) ground almonds (almond flour)
90 g (3¼ oz/¾ cup) plain (all purpose) flour

For the glaze:
60 g (2 oz/½ cup) icing (powdered) sugar
5 ml (1 teaspoon) culinary rose water
10 ml (2 teaspoons) passion fruit pulp

Preheat the oven to 190°C (375°F).

Line a large baking sheet (or several) with baking parchment.

Beat the butter and icing sugar together until soft and fluffy, then stir in the vanilla extract, rose water and passion fruit pulp. Beat the egg whites until frothy (not stiff) and stir into the butter mixture. Sift the ground almonds and flour together, then gently fold into the batter.

Take spoonfuls of the batter and spread into circles on the prepared baking sheet(s), each about 7 cm (2¾ in) in diameter and not too close together because they do spread a bit.

Bake for 8–10 minutes until the cookies are pale golden at the edges. Cool briefly on the baking sheets, then lift the cookies off carefully with a spatula and allow to finish cooling on a wire rack.

Make the glaze by combining the ingredients with enough water to make a smooth and thick glaze. Spoon a little glaze over each of the drops. You can also add a few crushed dried rose petals to the top of each cookie!

✷ WITCHY WISDOM

Apart from using flowers in baking you can also bring their magic into your kitchen. Simply arrange a few blooms in a jug on your altar or use essential oils in a burner or fragrant candle. Here are just a few possibilities:

- ◆ *Roses* – not just for romance but also for self-love, confidence, beauty and spiritual energies
- ◆ *Daisies* – well-being, simplicity, happiness and abundance
- ◆ *Jasmine* – good fortune, joy and release from worry and stress
- ◆ *Pansies* – clarity of thought, new ideas and self-understanding
- ◆ *Geranium* – protection against negative forces, emotional and physical healing of all kinds
- ◆ *Forget-me-not* – health, memory enhancement, quiet reflection
- ◆ *Nasturtium* – bright energy and health, freedom and increased creativity

THE KITCHEN WITCH

CORN & PEPPER BREAD

Lughnasad (1 August) is also known as Lammas, and was the original harvest festival, honouring and celebrating bread as the ultimate gift of Mother Earth, the source of life and nourishment. It's thus a particularly relevant day for kitchen witches of all kinds, for it celebrates the very heart of our magical practice: fire, grain and water, the elemental mysteries transformed into nourishment for body and soul. Even if bread baking is not part of your usual routine I invite you to try and make a simple loaf this year – even a quick bread, as in this recipe. This bread also includes corn and cornmeal, which are made with one of the seven sacred grains and have been used in rituals and as food for centuries, particularly in the Americas. Corn is linked to the ancestors, prosperity and protection – even a few dried corn kernels left on your kitchen altar will ensure only positive energies enter your home.

MAKES 1 MEDIUM LOAF, OR APPROXIMATELY 10 REGULAR MUFFINS

125 g (4½ oz/1 cup) plain (all purpose) flour
50 g (1¾ oz/⅓ cup) fine polenta (cornmeal)
5 ml (1 teaspoon) salt
15 ml (1 tablespoon) baking powder
65 g (2¼ oz/½ cup) finely grated Cheddar
2 eggs, beaten

125 ml (4½ fl oz/½ cup) cooking oil
250 ml (8 fl oz/1 cup) buttermilk
150 g (5½ oz/¾ cup) well-drained corn kernels
½ small red pepper, finely chopped
A few spring onions (scallions) sliced thinly
A small red chilli, chopped (optional)

Preheat the oven to 200°C (400°F).

Grease a medium bread/loaf pan very well. You can also make this bread in a muffin tin (pan).

Sift the flour, polenta, salt, baking powder and Cheddar into a large mixing bowl. In another bowl, beat together the eggs, oil and buttermilk. Stir this into the flour mixture, then add the corn, pepper and onions (plus chilli, if you are using it). Beat to make a thick batter – don't overbeat, a few lumps are okay.

Spread the batter evenly in the bread/loaf pan or divide it between the muffin tin holes. Bake in the oven for 20–25 minutes, or until a thin skewer or similar inserted into the loaf comes out clean. Cool on a wire rack for 10 minutes before turning out; this bread is at its best served fresh and warm!

✳ WITCHY WISDOM

Lughnasad is also the celebration of Lugh, the Sun god; the Sun is central to our lives here on Earth, and brings us warmth, light and a rich harvest of good things throughout the year. We should never forget to honour the Sun and its gifts to us – one simple way is by making a small bottle of Solar Magic Oil. Simply place 125 ml (4½ fl oz/½ cup) of olive oil in a small glass jar or bottle. Add a few sprigs of rosemary and some dry bay leaves, then seal the bottle and place on a cool, dark shelf. You can use a little of the fragrant oil in cooking for salad dressings and the like, or simply place a few drops on your forehead while saying the following simple mantra:

Sun, I bless and honour you.
Thank you for your light.
Bless our way forward with warmth
and joy.
And so it is.

APPLE & BLACKBERRY CAKE WITH ROSEMARY CRUMBLE

Mabon, the Autumn Equinox, takes place on or around 21 September, and is the second of the great harvest festivals, as well as being the traditional Pagan thanksgiving, a time to count our many blessings and share them with loved ones, friends and others we may not know at all. The ancient celebration of the harvest was a happy and joyful time, yet also balanced with the awareness that winter was just around the corner; it was a time to take stock of what had been accomplished and what still needed to be done or changed. The cake here is made with apples, a traditional Mabon food; blackberries are sacred to Lugh, the Sun god, who is also honoured at this time, and rosemary has powerful links to memory and tradition. It's perfect served at teatime or as a dessert at this liminal time of year.

SERVES 8-10

For the apple & blackberry cake:
125 g (4½ oz/1 cup) plain (all-purpose) flour
110 g (4 oz/¾ cup) wholemeal (wholewheat) flour
230 g (8 oz/1 cup) caster (superfine) sugar
10 ml (2 teaspoons) baking powder
5 ml (1 teaspoon) ground cinnamon
80 ml (2½ fl oz/⅓ cup) vegetable oil
180 ml (6 fl oz/¾ cup) milk
1 egg
5 ml (1 teaspoon) vanilla extract
3-4 small apples, peeled and cut into small chunks

15 ml (1 tablespoon) fresh lemon juice
150 g (5½ oz) fresh or frozen blackberries

For the rosemary crumble:
60 g (2 oz/½ cup) plain (all-purpose) flour
45 g (1½ oz/¼ cup) soft brown sugar
2.5 ml (½ teaspoon) ground cinnamon
65 g (2¼ oz/¼ cup) cold butter
15 ml (1 tablespoon) very finely chopped fresh rosemary leaves

Preheat the oven to 180°C (350°F).

Grease a 24-cm (9½-in) springform cake tin (pan) very well and line the base with baking parchment.

Sift both flours into a large bowl, together with the caster sugar, baking powder and ground cinnamon. Beat the oil, milk, egg and vanilla extract together in a small bowl until thick and smooth, then stir this into the flour mixture. Mix the chopped apples with the fresh lemon juice and stir into the batter. Spread the batter in the prepared tin and sprinkle the blackberries over the surface.

Make the crumble by mixing the flour, brown sugar and cinnamon together, then rub in the chilled butter until the mixture resembles fine breadcrumbs. Stir in the chopped rosemary.

Sprinkle the crumble evenly over the cake batter and bake for 40–50 minutes, until a thin skewer or similar inserted into the cake comes out clean. Cool in the tin for 15 minutes, then carefully loosen the sides of the tin and lift the cake off the base, peeling away the baking parchment. Leave the cake to cool on a wire rack.

✷ WITCHY WISDOM

If we are lucky enough to have food to eat, a kitchen to work in and shelter from the elements, we are already infinitely blessed. We can show our gratitude and thanks for these gifts by using our kitchens to spread our blessings outward; perhaps we can get together for bread-making sessions and then share them with others around us who might not be so fortunate. Or we can simply bake some bread and break it with loved ones in a mindful way; and please don't forget to keep some crumbs to throw out for the birds – like most kitchen witches I feed the birds on a daily basis and believe that they are messengers from other realms (however, that's a topic for another book!). Whatever we choose to do with our bread we should bless it with these simple words:

Blessings of grain, air, water and fire.
Blessings of bread.
May we always be fed with love
and with spirit and hope.
May we always remember to feed others
and share our abundant harvest.
Blessings and light ... and so it is.

CELEBRATING KITCHEN MAGIC

*'There is nothing ordinary in life,
because life itself is mystical, magical
and extraordinary ...'*

Debasish Mridha

Celebrate is often a word we think of in relation to the 'big' things –
special holidays and festivals, weddings and other major life events.
But to kitchen witches, all of life is (or should be) a celebration – for
every day is more than enough reason to celebrate the fact that we are
here on this beautiful Earth, sharing her gifts and enchantment with
those we love: family, friends, pets and the greater world around us.

In this final section I have chosen a few recipes that celebrate the gift
of life in various delicious ways; may their sweetness become part of
your kitchen magic and enchantment, too, as we turn each day into
one of joy, grace and abundance.

CERRIDWEN'S CAKE WITH EARL GREY SYRUP & ORANGE FROSTING

Cerridwen is a Celtic goddess of the earth, fire and cauldron – in fact, just about everything we do in the kitchen is linked to her on some level. This deep, dark cake is symbolic of the rich earth from which all life flows, while the orange flavours – both from the bergamot oil in Earl Grey tea and the fresh juice in the frosting – are linked to the Sun, the source of light and warmth.

SERVES 6-8

For the Earl Grey syrup:
250 ml (8 fl oz/1 cup) boiling water
2 Earl Grey tea bags
115 g (4 oz/½ cup) caster (superfine) sugar
Zest of 1 orange (optional)

For the frosting:
125 g (4½ oz/½ cup) soft butter
310 g (10½ oz/2½ cups) icing (powdered) sugar
1 egg yolk (optional)
65 ml (2 fl oz/¼ cup) fresh orange juice

For the cake:
125 g (4½ oz/½ cup) soft, unsalted butter
345 g (12 oz/1½ cups) caster (superfine) sugar
2 eggs
5 ml (1 teaspoon) baking powder
5 ml (1 teaspoon) bicarbonate of soda (baking soda)
A pinch of salt
60 g (2 oz/½ cup) (unsweetened chocolate) cocoa powder
185 g (6½ oz/1½ cups) cake (superfine) flour
5 ml (1 teaspoon) vanilla extract
200ml (7 fl oz/scant 1 cup) water

You can make the Earl Grey syrup in advance because it can be stored in a small glass jar in the fridge for several days. To make the syrup, pour the boiling water over the tea bags in a small saucepan and allow the tea to steep for 15 minutes. Remove the tea bags and add the sugar to the saucepan. Bring to the boil and simmer gently until the mixture is reduced by at least one-third and the syrup slightly thickened. Add the orange zest, if using, and allow the syrup to cool completely.

Preheat the oven to 180°C (350°F).

Grease two 23-cm (9-in) cake tins (pans).

Cream the butter and sugar together until light and fluffy, then beat in the eggs, one at a time. Sift together all the dry ingredients, then add to the butter mixture to form a thick batter. Lastly, add the vanilla extract and water, and beat well for two minutes.

Divide the batter evenly between the cake tins, and bake for 30–35 minutes, until the cakes are well risen and a thin skewer or similar inserted into them comes out clean.

Turn the cakes out onto a wire rack and leave to cool for 10 minutes. Drizzle 30–45 ml (2–3 tablespoons) of the Earl Grey syrup over the surface of each cake – they must not become too saturated.

While the cakes are baking, make the orange frosting: mix the butter and icing sugar together until thick and fluffy, then stir in the egg yolk (if using) and the orange juice; you may need to add a little more icing sugar if the frosting is too soft. Use half the frosting to sandwich the cake layers together, then swirl the rest decoratively over the top. A little of the remaining syrup can be drizzled over the cake, too.

Cover the cake and keep cool – it will stay fresh for 2–3 days.

✴ WITCHY WISDOM

This simple ritual is best worked on a Sunday – the day that honours the bright Sun. Bring some yellow flowers (particularly sunflowers or dandelions) into your kitchen, and also a bright yellow or orange candle. Place these on your kitchen altar, or just on the kitchen table if you prefer. Fill small fabric bags with a few cloves and cumin seeds, a little dried orange zest and a few drops of bergamot or neroli essential oil, then tie them up with yellow ribbon. Distribute the bags among all those present, or simply tie one around your wrist if you are alone, and say the following words (facing the Sun, if this is possible):

Thank you, Goddess of Earth and growth,
thank you, Sun, for your power and warmth.
May your heat and vitality always fill us
and may our light shine
with bright joy and goodwill to all.
And so it is.

ROSE BERRY CREAM PIE

Unbaked (apart from the crust), this creamy and delicious pie is given a delicate floral taste and fragrance thanks to the rose water, which is the traditional symbol of love and affection. The berries are also magically linked to deepening bonds of love and commitment, so this pie is wonderful served as part of a romantic evening celebration, or just to say 'I love you' to anyone who is a special part of our lives – after all, we often forget that friends, too, are part of the loving network that makes our lives such a magical gift!

SERVES 6-8

For the crust:
250 g (9 oz) shortbread biscuits, finely
    crushed
125 g (4½ oz/½ cup) melted butter
30 ml (2 tablespoons) sugar

For the filling:
15 ml (3 teaspoons) gelatine powder
200 ml (7 fl oz/scant 1 cup) water

385 g (13½ oz) can sweetened condensed milk
30 ml (2 tablespoons) rose water
5 ml (1 teaspoon) vanilla extract
250 ml (8 fl oz/1 cup) single (light) cream
250 g (9 oz) full-fat cream cheese
125 g (4½ oz) small strawberries and/or
    raspberries
Fresh rose petals or chopped pistachio nuts for
    garnishing (optional)

Preheat the oven to 170°C (340°F).

Grease a 23-cm (9-in) tart/pie dish (pan) lightly.

Make the crust first: place the crushed biscuits in a bowl, pour over the melted butter and sugar, and mix with a fork until the mixture resembles sand. Press the mixture evenly over the base and sides of the prepared tart/pie dish. Bake for 5-10 minutes until just golden, then remove from the oven and allow to cool completely.

To make the filling, mix the gelatine into the water in a small heatproof glass bowl (mixing with cold water before dissolving ensures there won't be any lumps in the finished mixture), then dissolve it over a pan or jug of hot water.

In a large bowl, mix the condensed milk, rose water, vanilla extract, cream and cream cheese together to make a smooth mixture. Add the dissolved gelatine and mix well. Stir in the berries, then spoon the mixture onto the biscuit crust. Chill for at least 3 hours until set; serve slices of the pie garnished with fresh rose petals or chopped pistachios.

✳ WITCHY WISDOM

Roses for a blessing – I first learned of this beautiful, yet simple ritual in Titania Hardy's lovely book *Titania's Book of House*, although I have changed it a little. It's particularly useful when we, or any loved ones, are feeling a little low, sad or generally lacking in romance in our lives. You will need roses – preferably white or pink, but any colour will do – one for each person present. Lay them out along your table and sprinkle each with a few drops of rose water. Say the following words quietly, after which each person present should take a rose and carry it home with them:

Love is our gift, our meaning, our heart.
May this rose be a powerful symbol
of the love we share, we give, we are blessed with.
And so it is and always will be.

The roses can also be dried and made into love bags by adding the petals to a small bag together with a few drops each of rose and lavender essential oil, as well as a small rose quartz crystal. Tie the bags with pale pink or mauve ribbons and hang from the head of your bed to have truly romantic dreams!

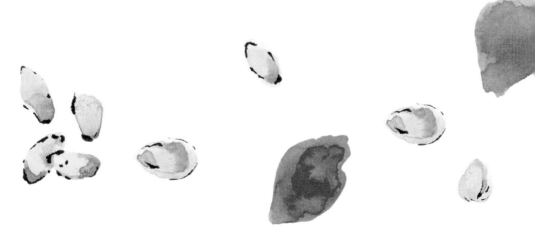

RAINBOW HERB BREAD

This is (very) loosely based on a traditional Scandinavian bread called *Smörgåstårta* because it was served as part of a smorgasbord buffet. However, this is my simplified, witchy version, made using a quick bread recipe. The cream cheese fillings can be adapted to suit what you like or have in your kitchen: these are simply a few suggestions! Bread is, of course, one of the most magical of all foods – the baking of bread symbolises the changes in our own lives and is kitchen alchemy at its deepest level. This recipe is ideal for any celebratory gathering at any time of the year and makes a good alternative for those who prefer savoury to sweet. The herbs you choose to use will also reflect your intentions with the bread – for example, thyme for healing and peace, chives for protection and positive energies, basil for prosperity or oregano for love and happiness. The wheat in the bread is full of solar energies, while the cheese cream in the filling has powerful links to the Moon.

SERVES 6-8

For the bread:
310 g (10½ oz/2½ cups) plain (all-purpose) flour
10 ml (2 teaspoons) baking powder
5 ml (1 teaspoon) salt
2.5 ml (½ teaspoon) black pepper
2.5 ml (½ teaspoon) mustard powder (optional)
45 g (1½ oz/¼ cup) finely grated Parmesan
2 eggs
65 ml (2 fl oz/¼ cup) light olive oil (or vegetable oil)
250 ml (8 fl oz/1 cup) buttermilk

For the filling and garnish:
500 g (1 lb 2 oz) cream cheese
65 ml (2 fl oz/¼ cup) crème fraîche or mascarpone

Plus your choice of the following flavourings:
15 ml (1 tablespoon) basil pesto and chopped fresh basil
Red pepper pesto and a little tomato purée/paste or smoked paprika
5 ml (1 teaspoon) mustard or 15 ml (1 tablespoon) hummus
Chopped herbs such as chives, dill or parsley for the top, together with chopped sundried tomatoes, olives or capers

Preheat the oven to 180°C (350°F).

Grease and line a deep 23-cm (9-in) bread/loaf pan.

Sift the dry ingredients into a large bowl, then mix the eggs, oil and buttermilk in another bowl. Stir this wet mixture into the flour mixture – you should have a thick, sticky batter.

Spread the batter evenly in the bread/loaf pan and bake for 40–45 minutes, until the bread is risen, golden brown and a thin skewer or similar inserted into it comes out clean. Cool in the pan for 5 minutes, then turn out onto a wire rack to finish cooling.

To make the filling, mix the cream cheese and crème fraîche together, then divide between four bowls. Depending on the flavourings you choose, you might need to add extra cream cheese if the filling is too runny.

Suggested flavourings:
Slice the cooled loaf evenly lengthways into three layers, then fill the layers with three of the flavoured cheeses; press together lightly, then top with the final flavoured cheese layer and sprinkle with fresh herbs or other garnishes as suggested in the list of ingredients.

Keep covered and chilled until serving time; use a long, serrated knife to cut thin, ribbon-like slices (no more than 5 mm/¼ in thick) from the loaf.

✹ WITCHY WISDOM

Before making bread (or indeed doing any baking) we can empower and bless our ingredients very simply and effectively. Lay the ingredients out in a circle and sprinkle a little salt right around the circle. Sprinkle a little flour around the salt circle and use your finger to draw small circles in the flour (these represent the Sun). Allow your own being to permeate and fill the circle – then say the following:

Sun, Earth and Moon,
bread and blessings.
We are fed, we are blessed,
may we always be nourished,
may we always nourish
each other and our beautiful Earth.
And so it is. Blessed be.

TRES LECHES COFFEE CAKE

Friends are truly a special gift in our lives and as such deserve to be given their own celebration; this large and luscious cake is perfect for sharing – serve it when you want to celebrate the unique and precious bonds of friendship! *Tres leches* cake is traditional to Mexico and South America, but it can be very sweet. I prefer this version, in which the sweetness is offset by the tang of the coffee, which is also magically linked to love and creativity, while the various milks are full of nurturing goddess and moon energies.

SERVES 8-10

---

5 large eggs, separated
230 g (8 oz/1 cup) caster (superfine) sugar
385 g (13½ oz) can evaporated milk
125 g (4½ oz/1 cup) cake (superfine) flour
7.5 ml (1½ teaspoons) baking powder
5 ml (1 teaspoon salt)

For the topping:
30 ml (2 tablespoons) good-quality
*   coffee granules*
30 ml (2 tablespoons) boiling water
385 g (13½ oz) can condensed milk
250 ml (8 fl oz/1 cup) single (light) cream
Cocoa powder (unsweetened chocolate)
*   for dusting*

Preheat the oven to 180°C (350°F).

Grease a 23 × 33-cm (9 × 13-in) rectangular cake tin (pan) well.

Beat the egg yolks and 170 g (6 oz/¾ cup) of the caster sugar together until light and thick. Fold in 80 ml (2½ fl oz/⅓ cup) of the evaporated milk, together with the flour, baking powder and salt.

Beat the egg whites in a large glass bowl until soft peaks form, then add the remaining caster sugar and beat until stiff. Fold the egg whites gently into the cake batter to make a thick, light mixture.

Spoon evenly into the cake tin and bake for 30 minutes, or until the cake is pale golden and a thin skewer or similar inserted into it comes out clean. Remove from the oven and leave to cool in the tin for 10 minutes.

For the topping, dissolve the coffee granules in the boiling water in a glass bowl; add the condensed milk and remaining evaporated milk, and stir well. Use a wooden skewer (or large fork) to poke holes evenly over the surface of the cake, then spoon the coffee topping evenly over the top, allowing it to sink in. Cover the cake and refrigerate until you are ready to serve. Before serving, whip the cream to soft peaks, then spread over the top of the cake and dust lightly with cocoa powder. The cake can be kept in the fridge for 2–3 days.

✳ WITCHY WISDOM

To further deepen the bonds of friendship you might like to try serving cups of this coffee blend (only to adults, if you add the brandy!) alongside the cake. Brew up a pot of your favourite coffee, then add a few cloves, the chopped rind each of an orange and lemon, and a few sprigs of rosemary (fresh or dried.) Steep the hot coffee for at least 20 minutes, then strain well and add a tot or two of brandy; serve in small cups and sweeten with a little honey, if desired.

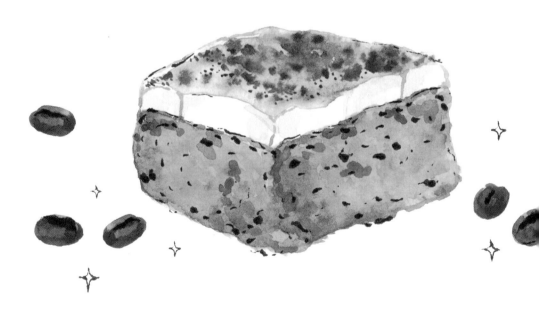

THE KITCHEN WITCH

PEACH, BERRY & MINT PAVLOVA

Deliciously light, fruity and creamy all at the same time – this pavlova makes a wonderful celebratory birthday dessert! The mint, berries, eggs and cream all have powerful lunar associations, which tie in perfectly with the whole birthday theme. For our birthdays are magical days: the day when we first arrived on this beautiful Earth and were given the gift of life. None of us should ever ignore or neglect to celebrate our birthdays – they are a magical part of our own personal calendars and give us the opportunity to celebrate not only what has been, but what is yet to come. Because of the moon magic in this recipe, it's lovely to serve this at night in a room lit only by candles – choose white, silver, violet or light blue candles to best reflect the moon's spirit. Or you can insert the candles into the cream and present this as a witchy birthday cake!

SERVES 6-8

For the pavlova:
4-5 egg whites, at room temperature
345 g (12 oz/1½ cups) caster (superfine) sugar
5 ml (1 teaspoon) white vinegar
5 ml (1 teaspoon) vanilla extract

For the topping:
65 g (2¼ oz/¼ cup) butter

115 g (4 oz/½ cup) caster (superfine) sugar
5 ml (1 teaspoon) vanilla extract
375 ml (13 fl oz/1½ cups) double (heavy) cream
4-5 ripe peaches, peeled and sliced
125 g (4½ oz) fresh berries of your choice (strawberries, raspberries, etc.)
A handful of chopped fresh mint leaves

Preheat the oven to 150°C (300°F).

Line a large baking sheet with baking parchment, then draw a circle measuring approximately 23 cm (9 in) on the paper.

Make the meringue by beating the egg whites until soft peaks form, then gradually add the sugar and continue beating until the mixture is thick and stiff. Fold in the vinegar and vanilla extract. Spread the meringue in a circle using the drawn circle as a guide, then build it up a little at the sides to create a shallow bowl shape.

Bake the pavlova for 2 hours, or until the meringue is very pale gold and lightly firm to the touch. Allow to cool completely.

While the pavlova bakes, make the topping: melt the butter, caster sugar and vanilla extract together over a low heat until a soft syrup is formed. Allow to cool.

The pavlova should only be put together shortly before serving, otherwise the meringue will soften. Whip the cream to soft peaks, then spread it in the meringue shell. Top the cream with the peach slices and berries (sliced if they are quite large), then drizzle with the cooled syrup and lastly sprinkle with the chopped mint.

✹ WITCHY WISDOM

Moon magic is just about the most potent kind there is; as kitchen witches we know and honour this, and a simple ritual reminds us of the power and significance of the lunar seasons and rhythms, rhythms that are echoed in our own bodies. Make this simple lunar oil (the recipe, which I adapted, comes from the late magical writer Scott Cunningham) by adding 6 drops of rose essential oil and 2 parts each of jasmine and sandalwood oil to a small bottle of base oil (125 ml/4½ fl oz/½ cup), such as sweet almond or jojoba. Place a few drops of oil on your wrist and forehead, and then say the following words:

Spirit of the Moon, I love and honour you.
Fill me with your light and magic
on every day and night of my life.
May I grow ever more magical and blessed
by your silver light and discover
the desires of my heart.
Blessed be and so it always will be.

FRANGIPANE TART

Self-care – which is basically just about valuing ourselves in body, soul and spirit as much as we value those around us – should be something we do every day, yet sadly we often put ourselves right down at the end of the 'to-do' list. Perhaps something as simple as sitting down with a cup of tea and a slice of homemade cake or tart can be the start of reconnecting with ourselves, and we should try and make this a regular part of our kitchen witchery. Magic is inextricably linked to healing on all levels, and so self-care, which balances us, is also an inevitable part of this magic, too. Just being with ourselves, in the moment, is key; it's also the ideal time to write in our kitchen grimoires, or perhaps consult a favourite pack of tarot or oracle cards, and see what messages they might have to share.

1-6 SERVINGS (OR INDIVIDUAL TARTS IF YOU PREFER)

For the pastry:
185 g (6½ oz/1½ cups) plain (all-purpose) flour
60 g (2 oz/½ cup) icing (powdered) sugar, sifted
125 g (4½ oz/½ cup) cold butter, cut into small pieces
5 ml (1 teaspoon) vanilla extract
1 egg
Cold water

For the filling:
125 g (4½ oz) ground almonds (almond flour)
30 g (1 oz/⅓ cup) self-raising (self-rising) flour
115 g (4 oz/½ cup) caster (superfine) sugar
185 g (6½ oz/¾ cup) butter
3 eggs
5 ml (1 teaspoon) almond extract
250 ml (8 fl oz/1 cup) strawberry or apricot jam/preserves
45 g (1½ oz/½ cup) flaked almonds (optional)

Preheat the oven to 180°C (350°F).

Grease a 20-cm (8-in) tart plate well; this recipe can also be made in a square 23-cm (9-in) cake tin (pan) and then cut into squares/bars to serve – in this case, simply press the crust evenly in the base of the cake tin, not up the sides.

Make the pastry by sifting the flour and icing sugar together, then rub in the butter until the mixture resembles coarse breadcrumbs. Stir in the vanilla extract and egg, then add enough water to make a soft, manageable dough.

Use your fingers to press the dough evenly over the base of the prepared tart plate; if it looks uneven, use a small glass to make the base smooth. Prick the pastry lightly with a fork, then bake for 15 minutes until pale golden brown. Leave to cool.

For the filling, sift together the ground almonds and flour. In another bowl, cream together the caster sugar, butter and eggs to make a smooth mixture. Add the almond extract, then stir this into the flour/ground almonds and beat well.

Spread the strawberry or apricot jam evenly over the cooled pastry base, then pour in the almond batter. Bake the tart for 30–40 minutes, or until the filling is risen and golden brown. Allow to cool on the tart plate, then sprinkle with the almonds, if using.

✳ WITCHY WISDOM

Gather a few supplies when you want to have a simple self-care ceremony: a white or rose candle, a dish of water, a rose quartz crystal and sandalwood essential oil (for balancing and calm). Sit quietly at your kitchen table and light the candle; sprinkle a little water over your hands and the crystal, then place 2–3 drops of the oil onto your wrists (ensure it has been added to a little base oil such as sweet almond before applying it to the skin). Say the following words softly:

I am me. I am well and strong.
I am deserving of love, and of
all good things ... blessings, grace and joy
in abundance.
I choose to honour and love myself,
as I do those around me.
And so it is.

KARPATKA

This is my version of a traditional Polish tart/dessert named for the Carpathian Mountains. I first tasted this at a magical food market in my hometown some years ago, made by a beautiful woman with red hair who looked as if she came straight out of a faerie tale. To this day, when I make this tart, I imagine I am making it in some beautiful castle in the middle of dark and mysterious woods, where all sorts of magic is afoot! However, I must be honest and say my version is not quite authentic, since proper *karpatka* has both top and bottom layers of choux pastry – mine only has one. I also use good-quality, shop-bought custard for the filling, since I find homemade custard sometimes has a tendency to get watery. Curiously, only after making this tart for several years did I discover, on a very old family tree, that I also have quite a few Polish roots ... magic, indeed.

SERVES 8-10

For the choux pastry:
250 ml (8 fl oz/1 cup) water
125 g (4½ oz/½ cup) butter, chopped
    into pieces
90 g (3¼ oz/¾ cup) cake (superfine) flour
2.5 ml (½ teaspoon) salt
4 large eggs
Icing (powdered) sugar, for dusting

For the custard and topping:
500 ml (17 fl oz/2 cups) vanilla custard
5 ml (1 teaspoon) vanilla extract
250 ml (8 fl oz/1 cup) single (light) cream
250 g (9 oz) dark chocolate, broken into pieces

Preheat the oven to 200°C (400°F).

Grease a shallow 26-cm (10-in) cake or tart tin (pan) very well.

Make the pastry by putting the water and butter in a medium saucepan and bringing to the boil. Once the mixture is boiling, stir in the flour and salt all at once and beat to make a thick paste. Take off the heat and cool for 5 minutes before adding the eggs, one at a time, and beating well after each addition. The pastry should be smooth and thick; spread it evenly over the base and up the sides of the cake/tart tin and sprinkle lightly with icing sugar.

Bake for 30–40 minutes; the pastry should be risen, golden brown and slightly crisp on top. Allow to cool in the dish.

To make the topping, beat the custard with the vanilla extract, then stir in half the cream, beating until stiff. Spread over the cooled pastry base. Place the remaining cream in a small saucepan and warm gently; stir in the pieces of chocolate and continue stirring until the chocolate has melted and the mixture is smooth and creamy. Cool for 10 minutes, then drizzle or pipe the chocolate ganache across the custard filling.

✳ WITCHY WISDOM

Whoever we are, we all come from somewhere; we all have ancestors and a background that stretches back through time and years. And this background is often linked to the making and sharing of particular foods and recipes: our kitchens are so often a place of memory and remembering, both of those who we still have with us and those passed from our sight. Perhaps this recipe will encourage you to seek out some traditional baking from your own family of origin and recreate it today ... I love this simple 'hand and a heart' ritual when baking something traditional from our family roots. You can perform this ritual holding hands with those physically present in your kitchen, or mentally holding those not present in your heart and spirit. Simply gather round and say the following:

Through food we remember and honour those
who came before us, those whose lives brought us our own.
With hands and in heart
We will always remember ... with love and respect.
Blessed be. And so it is.

GRIMOIRE NOTES

The first rule about keeping a grimoire is that there are no rules: they can be as simple or elaborate as we choose to make them. They can be written down in a basic exercise book, or created as a beautiful, illustrated journal – the choice is yours! You can also create an online grimoire if you prefer, as many people these days do – I'm a bit too old school for that!

The grimoire pages included in this book are for you to detail ideas, feelings and different kitchen experiments. Witches down the centuries have always been encouraged to keep a Book of Shadows, a way of recording and understanding personal magic, rituals and celebrations, and a kitchen grimoire is just an extension of that.

In it you can include your own recipes and notes or clippings, but even more importantly, you can record your own personal thoughts and experiences in your kitchen on a daily basis; as such the grimoire becomes not just a simple recipe book but a tool of inspiration and wisdom for your life's journey.

Blessings from one magical baker to another!

ACKNOWLEDGEMENTS

'Magic doesn't come from outside you.
It is part of you.
You can't weave together a spell
you don't believe in.'

Jim Butcher

I would like to thank Kate, Chelsea and all those at Hardie Grant for giving me the opportunity to write this book, on one of my favourite subjects! And to all those who have shared their baking skills and stories with me over many years – thank you too. Eternal gratitude to my mother, Catharine, for putting up with my kitchen experiments from a very early age, and also to Great-Aunt Rosie, who shared her baking wisdom with me – I miss you, but I also know you both continue to bake up a storm in the bright lands beyond the veil!

And to all those who believe in the magic, and know it starts in our hearts and spirits, often in the simplest of ways ...

Gail B.

ABOUT THE AUTHOR

Gail Bussi is a kitchen witch with Celtic and Italian heritage, and also a qualified herbalist, flower essence therapist and mindfulness coach; she has written three previous books on magical and natural living. She is also a designer, artist and baker, and has written on these subjects for various international publishers and magazines. Baking was her first love, as a young girl, and she has baked professionally and also run a small catering business.

Gail believes that the simple everyday rituals of home are the best way of finding the magic and spirit in our lives and her writing encourages this in a practical and accessible way.

She currently lives in a charming log cabin near the Eastern Cape Coast of South Africa, between mountains and sea, where she is surrounded by flowers, trees, herbs and lots of birdlife!

INDEX

Published in 2024 by Hardie Grant Books,
an imprint of Hardie Grant Publishing

Hardie Grant Books (London)
5th & 6th Floors
52–54 Southwark Street
London SE1 1UN

Hardie Grant Books (Melbourne)
Building 1, 658 Church Street
Richmond, Victoria 3121
hardiegrantbooks.com

British Library Cataloguing-in-Publication Data.
A catalogue record for this book is available from the British Library.

The Kitchen Witch
ISBN: 9781784886950
10 9 8 7 6 5 4 3 2 1

Publishing Director: Kajal Mistry
Senior Commissioning Editor: Kate Burkett
Senior Editor: Chelsea Edwards
Designer: Olivia Bush
Illustrations: Alice Mortimer
Copyeditor: Marie Clayton
Proofreader: Caroline West
Indexer: Helen Snaith
Production Controller: Gary Hayes
Colour reproduction by p2d
Printed and bound in China by Leo Paper Products Ltd.